SWITZERLAND

Patricia Levy/Richard Lord

BENCHMARK BOOKS

MARSHALL CAVENDISH
NEW YORK

PICTURE CREDITS
Cover photo: © Alamy Images: Peter Adams
alt.TYPE/REUTERS: 30, 41, 49, 50, 51, 52, 54, 74, 122 • ANA Press Agency: 5, 18, 29, 62, 76, 85 • China Tourism Photo Library/Anita C. K. Lee: 24, 26 • Corbis Inc.: 130 • Embassy of Switzerland: 3, 10, 19, 21, 28, 35, 55, 57, 67, 75, 79, 95, 98 (bottom), 107, 110, 111, 121, 124 • Focus Team Italy: 131 • HBL Network Photo Agency: 1, 4, 6, 46, 48, 53, 58, 61, 64, 84, 87, 104, 117 • Hulton-Deutsch Collection: 23, 25, 82, 83, 101, 102 (top and bottom) • Hutchison Library: 90, 98 (top) • Image Bank: 7, 12, 14, 39, 42 (top), 43, 45, 60 (bottom), 73, 81, 91, 96, 97, 119, 123, 126 (top and bottom), 128 • International Photobank: 15, 47 • Life File Photo Library: 13, 20, 31, 33, 40, 44, 63, 69, 70, 93, 106, 108, 120 • Lonely Planet Images: 16, 92, 114 • Buddy Mays: 8 • North Wind Picture Archives: 27 • David Simson: 37, 38, 56, 60 (top), 63, 77, 86, 89, 105, 109, 112, 115, 116, 125 • Bernard Sonneville: 66, 113 • Swatch: 42 (bottom) • Liba Taylor: 68, 71, 118

ACKNOWLEDGMENTS
Thanks to K.E. Battig von Wittelsbach of the Department of Romance Studies at Cornell University for her expert reading of this manuscript.

PRECEDING PAGE
Swiss children in traditional costume gather in a town in Zürich to celebrate an event.

Marshall Cavendish Benchmark
99 White Plains Road
Tarrytown, NY 10591
Website: www.marshallcavendish.us

© Times Media Private Limited 1996, 1994
© Marshall Cavendish International (Asia) Private Limited 2005
All rights reserved. First edition 1994. Second edition 2005.

® "Cultures of the World" is a registered trademark of Marshall Cavendish Corporation.

Originated and designed by Times Editions
An imprint of Marshall Cavendish International (Asia) Private Limited
A member of Times Publishing Limited

Library of Congress Cataloging-in-Publication Data
Levy, Patricia, 1951-
    Switzerland / by Patricia Levy. — 2nd ed.
        p. cm. — (Cultures of the world)
    Summary: "Explores the geography, history, government, economy, people, and culture
        of Switzerland"—Provided by publisher.
    Includes bibliographical references and index.
    ISBN 0-7614-1850-4
    1. Switzerland—Juvenile literature. I. Title. II. Series: Cultures of the world (2nd ed.)
    DQ17.L47 2005
    949.4—dc22   2004027508

Printed in China

7 6 5 4 3 2 1

3 1218 00379 6274

CONTENTS

A medieval warrior stands guard in front of a building in Stein am Rhein, northeast Switzerland.

A man from the canton of Vaud sits outside to enjoy the sun.

INTRODUCTION

SET AMID STUNNING MOUNTAIN RANGES and flanked on all sides by its neighbors, Switzerland is a country of enormous contrasts. From bustling urban centers and dynamic financial hubs, the visitor can travel in a couple of hours to tiny Alpine hamlets where villagers' lives revolve around raising livestock. Switzerland values its neutrality, yet has the most easily mobilized, highly armed, citizen soldiery in the world. Its industries range from high technology to textiles and tourism; its weather from areas of year-long snow to Mediterranean heat. In 700 years as a nation, Switzerland has produced important artists, writers, and thinkers, and has provided a safe haven for people forced to flee their own countries in times of war. This book, part of the *Cultures of the World* series, provides insights into the lives of the Swiss, how they work and play, their beliefs, culture, and aspirations. It offers a more detailed picture of Switzerland than what the average tourist may see.

GEOGRAPHY

LIKE ITS IMMEDIATE NEIGHBOR AUSTRIA, Switzerland is a landlocked country. It is bordered on the west by France, on the north by Germany, on the east by Austria and the tiny principality of Liechtenstein, and on the south by Italy. Switzerland is one of the smallest countries in Europe, both in terms of area and population. Covering 15,938 square miles (41,290 square km), it has a population of only 7,450,867, of which approximately 20 percent are non-Swiss resident immigrants. However, Switzerland's position at the center of Europe makes it a significant country. To the northwest of the country is the Jura mountain range, while to the southeast are the Swiss Alps. Between the two mountain ranges lies the Mittelland, the hub of the country where the bulk of the population lives.

Opposite: **Wooden chalets set in the mountains bear the burden of snow in the canton of Vaud.**

Below: **Besides drawing millions of skiers to the area every year, the Alps provide Switzerland with a vital resource—water. The country has more than a thousand lakes and many rivers.**

The Swiss Alps consist of a number of mountains, the highest of which is the Dufourspitze at 15,204 feet (4,634 m).

THE ALPS

The Alps are a crescent-shaped range of mountains beginning in southeastern France and extending across southern Switzerland into Austria. They are the largest mountain range in Europe. Three-fifths of Switzerland's landmass is covered by the Alps, but fewer than one-fifth of its people live there.

The Alps were formed in two stages millions of years ago. First, a period of mountain-building thrust up great arches of rock that buckled over and created the distinctive rock formations still visible today. A second episode of mountain-building pushed the whole chain even higher. Millions of years of erosion, followed by excavation by the great glaciers of the last Ice Age, created the complex shapes of today's Alps. The peaks of the Alps stood above the glaciers and were unaffected by them, but the glaciers filled the whole Mittelland region. Other glaciers carved out the valleys of the Alps. Where the glaciers finally disappeared, they left behind great mounds of debris that blocked the rivers and created the beautiful lakes of Switzerland.

AVALANCHES

When big masses of snow have their foundations loosened by rain or melted by warm winds, they begin to roll down mountainsides. These incidents are known as avalanches. Tremors caused by loud noises can also cause avalanches.

Avalanches are most likely to occur when the gradient or slope of the mountainside is more than 22 degrees. An avalanche can reach speeds of up to 245 miles per hour (394 km per hour). The air pushed along in front of the avalanche can cause as much damage as the avalanche itself, which may destroy buildings or even bury towns. Due to the size of an avalanche and the speed at which it travels, it is impossible to stop or alter its course. Between the years 2000 and 2004 approximately 87 people were killed in avalanches in Switzerland.

The Swiss Institute for Snow and Avalanche Research conducts studies and gives warnings about avalanches. Since World War II, the organization has produced reports on snow conditions during the winter months to warn snow skiers and mountain climbers of possible avalanches. The Institute uses a five-level warning system to rate snow conditions and the possibility of avalanches, from low to very high.

In addition, Switzerland has terrestrial and air mountain rescue teams that are on call 24 hours a day. Many artificial structures have also been built along the most susceptible stretches of roads and around Alpine villages to hold back the snow slides.

Today the Alps contain more than a thousand glaciers that are still at work carving out ever-deeper valleys. Compared to the great glaciers of the last Ice Age, however, these are tiny. The largest of them is the Aletsch Glacier, which is 14.6 miles (24 km) long and located near Bern.

The Alps are the source of many of Europe's major rivers. The high mountains with sharp inclines and the bountiful supply of water give Switzerland one of its greatest natural assets—hydroelectric power. The upper valleys of two rivers, the Rhine and the Rhône, divide the Alps into a northern and southern range of mountains. The appearance of the mountains varies according to the height and degree of exposure to winds. Up to 4,920 feet (1,500 m), the land is used for agriculture. Above this are coniferous forests. Above the tree line, the mountain pastures begin. Beyond 9,840 feet (3,000 m) little can grow, except a few mosses and lichens that cling to the bare rocks. The highest point in Switzerland is the Dufourspitze at 15,204 feet (4,637 m). The Matterhorn, with its distinctive outline, is slightly lower at 14,692 feet (4,481 m).

The hamlet of La Bosse lies 3,300 feet (1,006 m) above sea level on the high-lying plateau of the Jura Fribourg. Pastureland is more characteristic on the high plateaus of the Jura than cultivated fields, which are more commonly seen in the basins and valleys.

THE JURA

The Jura (YOOR-ah) covers 225 miles (362 km) of the French-Swiss border. The highest point of this mountain range is Crêt de la Neige (Mount Neige) in France, at 5,636 feet (1,718 m).

Jura is a Celtic word that means forest. The mountain range was formed by the same massive earth movements that built the Alps over a long period of time. It is thought that these upheavals, whose effects were felt all over Europe and beyond, were caused when the continents of Europe and Africa collided. The Jura are lower than the Alps. While the Alps are made up of a large variety of materials, the Jura mountains are more consistent and are made up of sandstone, limestone, and marl. They also contain many fossils, which tells us that a long time ago these mountains lay beneath a shallow sea. In fact, this mountain range gives its name to a period of geological time—the Jurassic. The fossils found in the Jura are believed to be remains of creatures from the Jurassic period.

While the peaks of the Alps escaped the rounding and weathering effects of the Ice Age, the Jura, being much lower, did not. Thus they are characteristically rounded in shape. The tops of the mountains are sparsely forested because they are above the tree line, but the valleys are wooded. Plateaus created by the erosion of the mountains provide good farming land. One such plateau, the Franches-Montagnes, lies just east of Switzerland's border with France.

While the Alps are cut through by the many river systems that give travelers easy access across the mountains, the Jura have few natural interruptions. This makes travel across them difficult, and the area has historically been a barrier to settlement.

The Mittelland is the backbone of the Swiss economy. Two-thirds of the country's population live in this region.

THE MITTELLAND

Deposits accumulated from the erosion of the Alps over millions of years gradually formed the Mittelland region of Switzerland. This large plateau was also carved by glaciers, but much more gently, to form rolling hills and valleys. Lake Geneva and Lake Constance were formed here as the glaciers hollowed out the lake beds and then melted, leaving the glacial deposits called moraines to block the paths of the meltwater. The Mittelland's average altitude is about 1,500 feet (457 m) above sea level.

The Mittelland makes up about 23 percent of Switzerland's landmass. It supports the greater part of Switzerland's population and is the base for Switzerland's economic success. Most Swiss cities are in this region.

RIVER SYSTEMS AND LAKES

Switzerland is considered the hydrographic center of Europe. Both the Rhine and Rhône, two of Europe's biggest rivers, have their sources here. The meltwater from the Alps and the Jura provides the starting point for these great rivers that so many countries in Europe depend on.

The Rhine rises in the Alps and flows first into Lake Constance. As it moves toward the lake, it carries meltwater and mountain streams with it. When it arrives at Lake Constance it is heavily burdened with debris, mud, and gravel. This material remains in the lake. The Rhine emerges again from Lake Constance a green and steady-moving river. The Rhine forms a natural boundary between Switzerland and Germany as far west as Basel, where it leaves Switzerland and begins its journey across Germany.

The Rhône rises in the Rhône glacier in the Furka Pass in the Alps, a few miles away from the source of the Rhine. It descends westward toward Lake Geneva, where it deposits all the material it has carried from the mountainside. At Lake Geneva, it leaves Switzerland behind and becomes a French river, traveling the rest of its journey south along the Jura mountains until it meets the Saône River.

Two other important rivers that have their sources in Switzerland are the Ticino, which flows south from the Alps, and the Reuss, which flows northward. The enormous potential power of Switzerland's glaciers and river systems has been effectively harnessed in power stations that use underground tunnels to carry water and generate electricity. Two of the highest dams in Europe are in Switzerland. They are the Mauvoisin Dam at 777 feet (237 m) and the Grande Dixence Dam at 935 feet (285 m). Both are on the higher reaches of the Rhône and are efficient sources of electrical power.

Lake Geneva is formed by the Rhône river. Prehistoric dwellings have been found on the shores of the lake.

The Swiss lakes are a major tourist attraction. Lake Geneva, also known as Lac Léman, is a crescent-shaped lake in the west of Switzerland that forms part of the border between Switzerland and France. It is the largest of Switzerland's lakes and is 9 miles (14 km) at its widest point. Several of Switzerland's larger cities are sited around the lake, including, of course, Geneva itself. A fleet of ships is maintained on the lake.

Lake Constance forms the eastern boundary of the Mittelland and Switzerland and part of the border with Germany and Austria. It is the second largest lake in Switzerland and is about 40 miles (64 km) long and 8 miles (13 km) wide. The lake's position along the borders gives it a long history as a center for smuggling, but today it is more important as a tourist center. Unlike many other Swiss lakes, it is not surrounded by mountains. The German town of Konstanz (Constance) sits right next to the Swiss town of Kreuzlingen, and border points between the two countries lie a short stroll from the center of both towns. In fact, Konstanz is the only German town on the southern side of Lake Constance.

MAJOR CITIES

Switzerland's largest city, Zürich, not only is more economically vibrant than the country's other cities but is also rich in intellectual life. Zürich is the home of the well-known Swiss novelist and dramatist Max Frisch.

ZÜRICH Although it is not the capital of Switzerland, Zürich (or Zuerich) is its largest city and the one that many people believe is the heart of Switzerland. The city is affectionately known to locals as Züri. The city is the economic, industrial, and cultural center of the country and has a population of more than 1.2 million. Zürich's Kloten Airport is a major international airline travel hub. The city's chief industries are banking and finance, commerce, engineering, electrical appliances, textiles, and tourism. Built around Lake Zürich and the river Limmat, Zürich has been a member of the Swiss Confederation since 1351.

BERN This is the federal capital of Switzerland, with a population of around 957,000. It too is a major industrial center, home to the pharmaceutical industry, the chocolate-making industry, and the printing trades. It has been a member of the Swiss Confederation since 1353. The older part of the city is perched high on a ridge, in a loop of the Aare River. Much of this medieval city is preserved and is a heritage center. Characteristic of the city's shopping centers are arcades that stretch out over the sidewalk, offering pedestrians protection against harsh weather.

GENEVA This city is built around Lake Geneva and the Rhône. Its major industries include banking, precision instruments, and chemicals. Geneva is the home of more than 200 international organizations, such as the Red Cross and some of the administrative sections of the United Nations. These organizations' employees, along with other foreign residents, make up a sizeable expatriate community in the city. Out of the 184,758 residents, 44 percent are foreign. Geneva has a long tradition of welcoming foreigners. In the 16th and 17th centuries many French Protestants fled to Geneva to escape persecution in their home country.

Bern's history is preserved in fine old streets and buildings. It is a historical center rather than a modern cultural one, and has many museums.

BASEL Situated on the borders of France, Germany, and Switzerland, and sited on the banks of the Rhine, Basel is an important center of commerce, communications, and chemical manufacturing. Pharmaceuticals, electrical engineering, and the manufacture of machinery and silk textiles are also important. It is the second largest city in Switzerland and has approximately 188,000 residents. Many of Switzerland's imported goods enter the country via Basel, being transported up the Rhine from Germany and beyond. Basel is a very prosperous city and is home to many of Switzerland's millionaires. The Rhine and its six bridges dominate the city, giving it an almost nautical air, as great barges ply up and down the river.

CLIMATE

Switzerland's climate varies from area to area because of the enormous differences in altitude and the effects of the mountains. As the land rises, temperatures fall by 3°F (2°C) for each 1,000 feet (305 m). In the Mittelland and Alpine valleys, the weather is damper and cloudier than above the cloud line in the high Alps, where the air is dry and there is frequent sunshine. The Swiss Alps have long been a choice location for sanatoriums, where people with various illnesses can recuperate.

In summer, the Mittelland is warm and sunny, with temperatures of 65 to 70°F (18 to 21°C). The sheltered valleys of the Jura and the Alps become hot during the summer months, while the upper slopes are cool. In the region of the Alps that extends toward Italy, the climate is more Mediterranean, with hot summers and mild winters. Switzerland has high precipitation, which falls as rain or snow. The Mittelland gets around 45 inches (114 cm) of rain per year, while in the higher areas 100 inches (254 cm) of rain per year is common. All precipitation is in snow form in areas above 11,500 feet (3,507 m).

The ibex is a large-horned mountain goat that can cling easily to rocky surfaces. It is an excellent climber and jumper and lives above the tree line most of the year.

FLORA AND FAUNA

One of Switzerland's greatest natural assets is its many thousands of forests. Fortunately for Switzerland, while other European countries cut down their native oaks and other trees for industry and firewood, the Swiss saw the value of planting.

Switzerland has both deciduous and pine forests. The deciduous forests grow largely in the Jura region, while the mountains of the Alps are covered in natural or planted forests of spruce, larch, and arolla pine trees. The larch is an interesting tree, for unlike the other conifers, it sheds its leaves in the fall instead of winter. Arolla pine trees can live for 400 years.

Many of the rarer plants of the Swiss Alps are protected by law. The edelweiss is a famous plant that grows high above the tree line in the mountains. It is normally 2 to 12 inches (5 to 30 cm) tall and has white woolly leaves and small yellow flowerheads. Other rare Alpine plants are the gentianella, the Alpine pansy, the aster, and the blue thistle.

Switzerland's wildlife is varied and beautiful. But with the encroachment of urban areas, greater use by tourists, and the Swiss love of hunting, many species have become endangered. In 1914 the Swiss National Park was formed in the Engadine area of Graubünden, and some degree of protection was given to the wild creatures of the area. Species of deer that were rare in the early 20th century have increased to the point where their presence now endangers the survival of some plant species. Ibex were wiped out entirely in the 19th century but were reintroduced and are once again wandering the slopes outside the Swiss National Park. The chamois, a small goat-like antelope, also lives freely in the Alps. It usually stands at a height of 30 inches (76 cm) and weighs 55 to 110 pounds (25 to 50 kg). The chamois has vertical horns, black and white markings on the face, and a black tail. It was hunted in earlier times for its soft skin, which was used to make clothing.

Wildflowers bloom in the Alpine valleys of Switzerland. The valleys are home to many plants, including the dandelion and the cornflower.

17

HISTORY

EVIDENCE OF HUMAN HABITATION in Switzerland dates back 30,000 years to the Paleolithic age. Humans subsisted by hunting animals and gathering wild plants. Cutting tools that probably belonged to Neanderthals have been found in Cotencher Cave in Neuchâtel. Later, people of the Neolithic age settled in the Rhône and Rhine valleys. They practiced agriculture and raised livestock. From 1,800 B.C., Bronze Age people settled in the Mittelland and Alpine valleys and shaped bronze and copper into tools and weapons.

By the late Iron Age, a great new center of culture had emerged on the banks of Lake Neuchâtel: the La Tène civilization of the Celts, a warlike race that swept across Europe. In what is now Switzerland, the Celts lived in the area between Lake Constance and Lake Geneva, on the Jura, and in the Alps.

Left: **Neuchâtel, the site of the Celtic La Tène civilization. The first Swiss coins came into existence during the La Tène civilization, around 800 B.C.**

Opposite: **Montebello Castle is one of several hillside castles in Bellinzona, in the canton of Ticino. The castle was built in the 13th century as part of the area's fortification efforts against external powers.**

19

A statue of Julius Caesar stands in the Roman Museum in Nyon, in the western canton of Vaud. Roman rule in Switzerland lasted 400 years.

UNDER FOREIGN RULE

By the time recorded history began, the Celts in Switzerland, called Helvetians, were facing border threats by powerful tribes from Germany. The Helvetians tried to emigrate to Gaul in an area that is now France. Unfortunately they found their way barred by the Romans under Julius Caesar, then governor of Gaul.

The Romans wanted the Helvetians to stay where they were to provide a barrier between the Roman Empire and the waves of invading Germanic peoples. In March 58 B.C. the Romans stopped the Helvetians at ancient Bibracte in Burgundy (France) and defeated them. The Helvetians were forced to retreat to what was to be called Helvetia (hehl-VAYT-see-ah), the area between Lake Constance and Lake Geneva. They were promised protection from the Germanic peoples by the Romans, and Helvetia became a province in the massive Roman Empire. Under the Romans, Helvetia developed rapidly. Road networks were built, towns were reestablished, and agriculture flourished.

A region to the east of Helvetia was inhabited by people who were related to the Etruscans and Celtics. Following Roman conquest of this area, spoken Latin mixed with the area's existing languages, resulting in a Rhaetian version of vulgar Latin. Through the centuries, this language has developed to become what we know as today's Romansh.

Switzerland was very important to the Romans. The borders of the Roman Empire lay north of Switzerland along the Rhine and Danube rivers, and the mountains of Switzerland formed a land barrier that troops could fall back to if the Germanic peoples advanced. Cities developed, notably Aventicum, the modern Avenches where ruins of Roman palaces, temples, and triumphal arches have been excavated.

Germanic peoples began invading Switzerland in A.D. 259, and Roman rule in the country finally crumbled in A.D. 400. The Celts were displaced by Germanic peoples, mainly Burgundians and Alemannians. The Burgundians settled in the western part of Switzerland. The vulgar Latin spoken in this area gradually evolved into a French dialect. This area is in the French-speaking section of present-day Switzerland. The Alemannians settled in the northern part of the country, which is the German-speaking section of Switzerland. The Rhaetians resisted the Alemannians and remained in Graubünden canton until today. The southern parts of Switzerland came under the influence of Italy. Hence four different power groups developed, each with its own language.

In the sixth century, Switzerland became part of the Frankish kingdom ruled by Clovis, the first Germanic king to convert to Christianity.

By A.D. 800, Switzerland was part of the Holy Roman Empire under Charles the Great, later called Charlemagne. It was under his rule that the modern cantons of Switzerland were largely created. By A.D. 843, Switzerland was split among Charlemagne's grandsons. It was not until 1032 that the Swiss territories were once more brought under a single ruler, the Holy Roman Emperor Conrad II. During the 12th century, Switzerland was again divided up and fought over. By 1291 Switzerland had come under the power of the House of Habsburg, which was to rule the Holy Roman Empire for nearly 400 years.

The Roman legacy can still be seen in many structures that are scattered across Switzerland. Networks and structures such as this viaduct were constructed to facilitate the movements of people, animals, and goods.

21

The House of Habsburg, also known as the House of Austria, was one of the ruling houses that dominated Europe from the 15th to the 20th century. The name Habsburg came from a castle named Habichtsburg (Hawk's Castle), which was built in 1020 in Aargau, Switzerland.

THE FOUNDATION OF MODERN SWITZERLAND

As an outcome of the increased power of the Habsburgs, a desire for autonomy and freedom was born in some of the cantons that would later become Switzerland. For the first time they saw a common goal of independence from emperors.

In 1291 Emperor Rudolf of Habsburg died, and in the vacuum created by his death, some of the Swiss cantons decided to act. Three of them, Uri, Schwyz, and Unterwalden, drew up a defense agreement called the Perpetual Covenant, pledging mutual aid and allegiance. Guerrilla attacks were made on the bailiffs and soldiers of the Habsburg Empire. One of the Habsburg dukes led a force against the united cantons in 1315 but was defeated by them. This led to a whole spate of other cantons joining the Confederation—Lucerne in 1332, Zürich in 1351, Glarus and Zug in 1352, and Bern in 1353. The Swiss fought and defeated the Habsburgs in 1386 and 1388.

THE EARLY CHRISTIANS

One of the first groups of Christians to arrive in Switzerland was a band of Irish monks, led by Columban, in A.D. 610. An early chronicle described the monks as long-haired and tattooed, carrying stout sticks, and a spare pair of boots around their necks. They traveled around Switzerland throwing carved images of gods into the rivers and causing havoc among the population, who resented their high-handed attempts to Christianize them. Driven out of the lakeside village of Tuggan, they moved into Brigantium (modern Bregenz) and began to smash heathen gods. Again ordered out of the area, the monks moved into Italy, leaving behind one of their number, Gall, who was too sick to make the journey. In A.D. 612 Gall founded a monastery on the site of the present-day Saint Gall.

WILLIAM TELL

No one can quite decide whether William Tell is Swiss history or Swiss myth. Whichever it is, it is a good tale and one that is as much a part of the character of Switzerland as Swiss cheese or cuckoo clocks.

William Tell's story begins during Emperor Rudolf's reign. His canton was governed by the ruthless Habsburg supervisor Gessler, who, the story goes, put his hat on a pole in the town center and made everybody who passed that spot bow to it. He also confiscated land from the Swiss, robbing them of huge sources of income in rents and tithes, and insulted them. When William Tell refused to bow to the hat, a series of insults between the two men led to Tell having to shoot an apple off his son's head *(above)*. Tell, who was known for his excellent aim, knocked the apple off with no injury to his child, but told Gessler that his second arrow would have been for him had his son died. This infuriated Gessler, who had Tell arrested. En route to jail, Tell escaped and ambushed Gessler, who got his comeuppance in the form of Tell's spare arrow through the heart. Tell became a national hero and a Swiss symbol of freedom.

Events from the history of Lucerne and the Swiss Confederation are depicted in a series of triangular tableaux between the rafters of the Chapel Bridge in Lucerne.

THE SWISS CONFEDERATION IN THE 15TH CENTURY

The Confederation of eight Swiss states began to look on expansion as their best defense. In the early 15th century, they took more land from the Habsburg Empire, while other Swiss cantons decided to declare their own independence without joining the Confederation. This group negotiated a temporary peace with the Habsburgs and instead took land from the Burgundian Empire. War against Burgundy began in 1474. In March 1476, a Burgundian army was defeated by a Swiss force at Grandson, and later that year in Morat, both towns in western Switzerland. Throughout the war, the reputation of the Swiss as soldiers grew. But as the Confederation took more and more land, they began to quarrel among themselves. In 1481, on the verge of civil war, they signed a new pact and drew two new cantons into the Confederation. Now a Confederation of 10 states, they were joined in the next 30 years by three more.

The Confederation began to grow rich, partly on the spoils of the many battles its mercenaries began to undertake on behalf of foreign kingdoms. Although Switzerland today stands for neutrality, for many years there were no major wars in Europe that did not have Swiss soldiers fighting on one side or another. The chief export of Switzerland became soldiers, and as their military prowess grew, so did the wealth of the city cantons. But this was not to last. Other countries learned the lessons of the Swiss mercenaries and set up competing mercenary forces. Warfare underwent a massive change during this century, and the high cost of military equipment began to make the prospect of peace more financially rewarding to European rulers.

THE REFORMATION

At the start of the 16th century things were in decline for the Swiss Confederation, which now consisted of 13 states and several occupied territories. Their reputation as mercenaries had declined, there was less demand for troops all over Europe, and they had been badly defeated by the French in the battle of Marignano in 1515.

Protestant reformer Huld-rych Zwingli is given a sad but rousing send-off by his supporters as he leaves Zürich.

Worse was to come in the form of the Reformation. It established the division between politics and religion in Europe and wrought dramatic changes all over the continent. None, however, were as affected as Switzerland.

The Reformation, led by Martin Luther in Germany, was a crusade against what was seen as corrupt practices in the Roman Catholic Church. Chief among these were the way in which the Church involved itself in secular matters, its financial corruption, and the ceremonies and furnishings of the Church itself that had become ostentatious, with the acquisition of paintings, statues, and valuable artifacts.

In Switzerland, the reforms were led by Huldrych Zwingli (HOOLD-ryke TSVING-lee), who saw the religious changes as part of a larger picture, the reform of society, starting in Zürich. He believed that in order to build a new society, it was necessary to destroy the old one. Zürich had long had a very bad reputation, and the city council was pleased to encourage him in his reforms. All decorations were thrown out of the churches, and in 1523 the Catholic rites were abolished in favor of Protestant services. The rural cantons surrounding Zürich did not go along with these changes and issued warrants for Zwingli's arrest. This led to war between the city's forces and the rural cantons in 1531. In the ensuing battle Zwingli was killed.

The Lion of Lucerne monument commemorates the heroism of those Swiss guards who were slain while defending the Tuileries Palace in Paris in 1792.

JOHN CALVIN In Geneva, another reformer called John Calvin was influential. His religious beliefs were more extreme than Zwingli's and concentrated on the church alone rather than interfering in state affairs.

The shock waves of the Reformation continued to affect Europe for another century. Before the end of the Reformation, there was one last destructive convulsion. This was the Thirty Years' War, a series of wars fought first over religion and later for territory and power. Although the Swiss Confederation remained neutral, the basic divisions that had opened up between the Protestant urban cantons and the rural Catholic ones meant that the cantons supported different parties in the wars.

When the Thirty Years' War ended in 1648, the rest of Europe acknowledged Switzerland as an independent confederation of states. The 17th and 18th centuries were marked by industrialization, which brought economic prosperity to Switzerland. The neutrality that the Swiss maintained during the Thiry Years' War helped to safeguard their economy. Refugees who fled to Switzerland also contributed to the economic growth, because they brought with them useful skills in watchmaking and textiles.

THE FRENCH INVASION

In 1798, during the French Revolution, French military forces invaded Switzerland under the leadership of their emperor, Napoleon Bonaparte. Switzerland became a French satellite state and was named the Helvetic Republic. Internal discord, however, brought about the demise of the Republic, which lasted only five years.

In 1803 Bonaparte enforced a settlement on the Republic, giving it some sovereignty and enlisting six of the previous vassal states as members.

These 19 cantons formed the Helvetic Confederation. In 1815, after more wrangling between the cantons, three more of the vassal states became full members of the Confederation. By now there were 22 cantons in the Confederation. It was during this period, too, that Switzerland's neutrality was recognized internationally.

A NEW CONSTITUTION

Starting in 1830, liberal constitutions were drawn up in 12 cantons. The year 1847 saw the end of a brief civil war between the Catholic cantons and the other Swiss cantons. The Catholic cantons broke off to form a separate government called the Sonderbund. In 1848 this dispute resulted in the drawing up of a new constitution. The rest of Europe continued in a state of turmoil for much of the 19th century, while the Swiss Confederation had finally found a means of peacefully coexisting, yet remaining neutral in European and world affairs. The last canton to join the Confederation was the Jura in 1974.

The Saint Gotthard Pass is an important road and railway route in the Alps between central Europe and Italy. Beneath the pass is the Saint Gotthard Tunnel, which is 10 miles (16 km) long and is one of the longest tunnels in the world.

SWISS NEUTRALITY AND THE TWO WORLD WARS

With many clearly differentiated cultural groups, Switzerland's neutrality and even its existence as an independent state was continually at risk. During the Franco-Prussian War of 1870–71, German Swiss supported Prussia, while French Swiss supported France. In 1914 the assassination of Archduke Ferdinand, which set in motion a chain of events that resulted in World War I, brought all the French-German tensions back to the forefront of Swiss life. Shortly after the war began, Swiss neutrality was threatened when it was discovered that German sympathizers were passing military secrets to the German side. The Swiss soldiers who patrolled the borders were not compensated for their lost wages. The Swiss economy felt the pinch of the war. Large numbers of refugees fled into Switzerland.

After the war, with its neutrality intact, Switzerland faced the dilemma of whether it could remain neutral and still join the newly formed League of Nations, the predecessor of the United Nations. Switzerland finally joined the League in 1920 as one of its original members. The seat, or headquarters, of the organization was moved to Geneva later that year and remained there until the League disbanded in 1946.

When World War II began to take shape, Switzerland was given special dispensation to ignore any trade sanctions against Germany. For the duration of the war, Switzerland traded with both the Allies and the Axis powers. Its borders were patrolled by 650,000 troops, and the Alps became the designated spot where German invading troops would be met and stopped. Switzerland planned to have its key facilities blown up should a German invasion occur. The Saint Gotthard Tunnel, a major artery through the Alps, was one of the facilities earmarked for destruction. Although German plans for an invasion of Switzerland were later discovered, it never took place, and Switzerland emerged from World War II with a booming economy among the ruins of the rest of Europe. It was thus perfectly placed to benefit from the enormous needs of reconstructing Europe. After World War II, Switzerland reverted to complete neutrality by refusing to join the United Nations, since doing so would mean possible involvement in military commitments.

Formerly the headquarters of the League of Nations, the Palais des Nations in Geneva today houses offices of the United Nations. Switzerland is a member of many international organizations, including the United Nations Educational, Scientific, and Cultural Organization (UNESCO) and the International Labor Organization (ILO).

Nonetheless, some important UN agencies were based in Geneva, and in 2002 Switzerland finally dropped its longstanding reservations and became a full member of the United Nations.

In more recent times, Switzerland has experienced other challenges to its stability. It became one of the last European states to grant women the vote, experienced a huge influx of foreign workers and refugees, and has met the challenges of the growing economies of Japan and Germany. It now faces the serious challenge of entry to the European Union. If Switzerland does not join the European Union, it will suffer economic isolation, but if it does join, its neutrality will be compromised. Either way, whether by economic pressures or by the dissolution of its sense of statehood as it accepts more and more regulations determined in Brussels, the EU headquarters, Switzerland's future seems set for a major change.

GOVERNMENT

THE SWISS SYSTEM OF GOVERNMENT today is very much the same as that set up by the country's 1848 Constitution. It has a Federal Assembly consisting of a bicameral legislative body. The two houses are the National Council, similar in function to the U.S. House of Representatives, and the Council of States, similar in function to the Senate. The National Council has 200 members elected for a four-year term by proportional representation, and the Council of States has 46 members selected by the cantons.

Above: The Confederation Center in Geneva. Geneva is the headquarters of many public and private international organizations.

Opposite: An aerial view of the Swiss Federal Parliament Building in Bern, western Switzerland.

An executive body called the Federal Council is elected every four years. It is known abroad as the Cabinet. Every year, a new president of the Federation is chosen from among the members of the Federal Council. The president's job is largely ceremonial.

Each canton is a sovereign state with its own government consisting of an executive and a legislative body. These state governments are responsible for education, public health, police, and local taxes.

Although elections to all these bodies take place every four years, the Swiss voter probably has more selections to make than in any other democracy. Referenda are common occurrences, with voting and elections held on weekends to cause as little disruption as possible.

THE CONSTITUTION

Before 1848 the Swiss Confederation consisted of a loose organization of 25 independent cantons, each with its own system of government, ranging from democracy to oligarchy and aristocracy.

The 1848 Constitution set up a Republican government in the middle of restored European monarchies. It gave control of foreign affairs to the federal government, imposed democratic government on all the cantons, and banned the hiring out of mercenary armies.

The Constitution was revised in 1874 and has been adjusted many times by referendum. The Constitution was fully revised in 1999 and implemented in January 2000.

THE FEDERAL COUNCIL

The highest authority is the Federal Council. Each of its seven members is responsible for a government department—defense, transportation and energy, justice and the police, the economy, finance, foreign affairs, and the interior. Three of the political parties are represented by two seats each, while the fourth has one seat. No two members can come from the same canton. In 1984 the first woman was elected to the council.

THE LEGAL SYSTEM

In 1912 the Swiss Civil Code went into effect, and since then many parts of it have been adopted wholesale by other countries setting up their own civil laws. The cantons run their own courts, with those convicted having access to the Federal Court of Appeal. Capital punishment was abolished in 1937 in all the cantons.

The first woman to be elected to the Federal Council was Elisabeth Kopp. She represented the canton of Zürich and served from 1984 to 1989. Kopp is a member of the Free Democratic Party.

CIVIL RIGHTS IN SWITZERLAND

Switzerland is a signatory to the European Convention on Human Rights, and each citizen's rights are laid down by both federal and cantonal law. The Constitution guarantees freedom of property ownership, freedom of trade and commerce, freedom of choice of domicile and worship, freedom of the press, consumer protection, and rights of association and petition. All men and, since 1971, women age 18 and above have the right to elect their representatives and to take an active part in deciding on legislation.

The right of initiative enables any citizen to propose a change to the Constitution. If 100,000 electors sign a proposed constitutional change, the federal government can make a counterproposal and a popular vote is taken on the issue.

The citizens also have a right to demand a referendum on any new piece of legislation. If 50,000 electors or eight cantons demand a referendum within 100 days of a new piece of legislation being published, the referendum will be held. If the voters decide against it, the legislation is dropped or altered.

A protest march on a street in Zürich. The Swiss actively exercise their democratic rights.

THE FEDERAL COURT

The Federal Court is the supreme arbiter of justice in Switzerland and is based in Lausanne. Its function is mainly as a court of appeal on judgments passed by the cantonal courts. Its judgments on cases become the law of the land. Other judges at lower levels must use the Supreme Court's judgments as models for their own. The Federal Court also arbitrates disputes between the cantons.

CANTONS AND STATES

In the chapter on history, the words canton and state were used as alternatives for the same political unit, but that is not quite right in the modern context. In present-day Switzerland, there are 23 states but 26 cantons. Three of the original cantons were divided up. Unterwalden, one of the three original signatories to the Confederation, was divided in the 12th century into Obwalden and Nidwalden, while Appenzell was divided into Appenzell Outer Rhodes and Appenzell Inner Rhodes in 1597, and Basel into Basel-City and Basel-Country in 1833. Each of the demicantons has its own independent regional government, but only half the voting power of the other full cantons in the federal government.

Within each canton, a government of around seven members is elected. Besides the government, the canton also has a parliament with one chamber. The number of representatives varies with each canton. Parliamentary elections are held on average every four years, again depending on the canton. The parliaments are empowered to collect taxes and decide on matters of education and social services.

At the administrative level below the canton, Switzerland is divided into 3,000 communes, each with its own local authority. Each commune has its own assembly, which anyone can attend to elect authorities or even take part in the running of affairs. The commune is responsible for the upkeep of public property such as forests, water, gas and electrical power, bridges, roads, administrative buildings, fire departments, and many other local services.

The size of each commune varies greatly. Some of them are larger than the small cantons; others are tiny. A Swiss individual remains permanently a member of the commune where his or her father was born, but when a woman marries, she joins her husband's commune.

THE LANDSGEMEINDE

The Landsgemeinde (LAHNTS-geh-min-de), an outdoor assembly of people gathered for the purpose of conducting government business, is an ancient tradition dating back to the 14th century. Once, all the cantons elected their leaders in this way, but now it is practiced in only one canton and one demicanton. Every spring, on the last Sunday in April or the first Sunday in May, the voters of Glarus and Appenzell Inner Rhodes hold an open-air meeting in the main squares of their capital towns to vote on a host of local issues. The residents may vote on the legislation, judges and cantonal representatives, permits, infrastructure, and so on. Voting is by a show of hands.

In the demicanton of Appenzell Inner Rhodes, the Landsgemeinde is a festive day. The town square, where the voting takes place, is decorated with colorful flags. There are also stalls selling special Landsgemeinde pastries. The event starts with a church service.

The Landsgemeinde, the constitutional assembly of free citizens, is held in the open in Glarus.

POLITICAL PARTIES

A two-party political system, such as is found in the United States, does not exist in Switzerland. We have seen that as a matter of custom each party is represented on the Federal Council so no one political group can really dominate or determine policy. There are different parties represented in the National Council, ranging from the larger groups, such as Christian Democrats, Radical Democrats, Social Democrats, and Swiss People's Party, to environmentalist groups and independents. The fact that the parties are able to cooperate so easily in government shows that they have very few major differences.

In addition to this type of political grouping, the system allows for pressure groups to form. Because of the citizens' rights to call for a referendum on national issues, groups form continuously in order to force discussion on certain topics. Conservationists, the anti-nuclear lobby, anti-fascist groups, and anti-abortion groups have all used their rights to call for a referendum on the issues they think are important.

FOREIGN POLICY

Switzerland long ago came to realize that, surrounded as it was by potential aggressors, its safest form of defense was neutrality. Switzerland's neutrality was accepted at the 1815 Congress of Vienna and in the 1919 Treaty of Versailles. But neutrality is not an easy position to hold in a world where increasingly countries are forming alliances in order to survive. Switzerland cannot enter any international agreement that might oblige the country to come to another's aid. It is not a part of NATO and became part of the United Nations only in 2002. Even now, Switzerland is not yet a part of the European Union. This is partly due to the country's desire to protect its domestic industries but even more so due to its political need to remain neutral.

Although Switzerland does not take sides in international disputes, the country puts a great deal of effort into its foreign policy. Switzerland spends huge sums on international aid to developing countries and has a relief corps that is dispatched to any natural disaster. Switzerland also provides an international service via the International Red Cross, maintaining a fleet of aircraft to be dispatched anywhere in the world where there are war casualties. During World War II, Switzerland opened its borders to 300,000 refugees. Geneva is also home to many international organizations that are involved in human rights and humanitarian international law, such as the World Health Organization (WHO). In addition, Switzerland maintains political relations with as many countries as possible and often acts as a go-between or mediator between countries that have cut off political relations with one another but still need to communicate.

Over the years, however, many people have criticized Switzerland's stance on neutrality, which has often proved to be lucrative. While their neighbors were at war, Switzerland has traded with both sides. It has been said too that Switzerland's banks have provided safekeeping for many a rogue's ill-gotten gains.

Swiss army tanks patrol the streets. The Swiss army is a militia, that is, it is made up of citizen soldiers rather than professional ones.

THE ARMED FORCES

To protect their neutrality, the Swiss make sure they can defend the country against invasion. To this end, all able-bodied men between the ages of 20 and 42 are permanently on call for national service, and officers undergo further training courses until age 52. All men undergo a basic training program, followed by supplementary annual training.

Women who are interested may join the military as volunteers. In addition, huge amounts of money have been spent providing the population with underground shelters in case of nuclear war between Switzerland's neighbors. Each soldier keeps his or her own weapons at home, ready for action. When war broke out in 1939, the Swiss Army mobilized 650,000 soldiers to protect its borders. During the battle of France in 1940, Germany violated Switzerland's neutrality by sending warplanes into Swiss airspace. They were shot down, and the incursions stopped.

ECONOMY

CONSIDERING THAT IT has huge disadvantages in terms of raw materials, transportation, land, and even population, Switzerland has done very well over the years. It has one of the highest standards of living in the world and had exports worth $110 billion in 2003.

Beginning in the Middle Ages, Switzerland's chief export was a group of well-trained soldiers who would fight for whichever king paid them the most. Switzerland grew rich on the spoils of war. After the battles of Grandson and Morat in 1476, when the Swiss routed the

Burgundian armies, huge hauls of booty were taken that included enormous diamonds, silks, and plain hard cash. Swiss neutrality in later years ensured that these resources were never lost.

During the Thirty Years' War in the 17th century, the Swiss grew rich by trading with the belligerents, supplying cereals, vegetables, and meat to countries so war-torn that they could not grow their own food. Switzerland also took in refugees whose skills began the Swiss tradition of producing tiny intricate objects such as watches and jewels.

Today Switzerland has thriving banking, watchmaking, chocolate, tourism, chemical, engineering, and pharmaceutical industries. Building on its centuries-long pedagogical tradition, Switzerland is also famous for a great number of international educational institutions. Students from all over the world attend these schools.

Above: **Swiss chocolates are world-renowned. Chocolate factories such as this one make hundreds of varieties of chocolates in all shapes and sizes.**

Opposite: **Credit Suisse is one of the largest banks in Switzerland. Many foreign investors are attracted by the country's banking system.**

Agriculture in Switzerland is characterized by fodder crops and grazing. Cattle, horses, pigs, and sheep are raised, and dairy products are important to the economy.

AGRICULTURE

Two-thirds of Switzerland's landmass is rock, water, or forest. Urban growth uses up another large chunk of the potential agricultural land so that only 11 percent of the total land surface is used for agriculture.

The number of people involved in agricultural production has declined rapidly. In the 19th century, 60 percent of the population worked in agriculture. By World War II, this had dropped to 22 percent, and it is now less than 5 percent. This does not mean, however, that agricultural production has dropped. Farms are now much larger than they once were and are highly mechanized. Agriculture contributes 1.5 percent of the GDP.

In the mountain regions, the chief activity is raising livestock, mostly cattle. In the central plateau and lower Alpine valleys, grapevines, vegetables, and tobacco are grown in addition to livestock. Dairy production dominates Swiss agriculture. Milk production is at a surplus, and cheese and chocolate, both milk products, are exported. Swiss vineyards produce an average of 127 million quarts (120 million liters) of wine every year. Grapes are grown in Ticino, the valleys of the Rhône, and near Lake Geneva, Lake Neuchâtel, Lake Biel, and Lake Zürich.

Many agricultural products are protected by the government against cheaper imports by means of import tariffs, and fixed prices paid to farmers for certain agricultural products. This need to protect the domestic agricultural industry is one of the chief reasons Switzerland has been reluctant to be a part of the European Union.

MACHINERY AND ELECTRONICS

The machine, electronics, and metallurgical industries account for a major part of Switzerland's total exports. About 26 percent of the total workforce is employed in these industries. The Swiss machine industry includes everything from machine tools and precision instruments to heavy electrical equipment. The machine tool industry originally developed out of the needs of Switzerland's own textile industry, which peaked during the 19th century. The development of railways, hydroelectric power, and the motorization of seagoing vessels all called for complex machinery, which was developed in Switzerland. The Swiss built the first electric track railway, the first turbo-generator, the first pump turbine, and the first gas turbine power station. As electronics have become more important in industry, Swiss technology has kept pace.

Switzerland is constructing the new Gotthard and Lötschberg base tunnels under the Alpine mountains to meet the expanding needs of the rail freight industry. The tunnels run underneath 8,202 feet (2,500 m) of rock. When completed, the Gotthard base tunnel will be the world's longest at 35 miles (57 km).

CHEMICALS AND PHARMACEUTICALS

The Swiss chemical industry, like the machine tool industry, developed out of the needs of the textile factories of the 19th century. Dyes were needed for the woven cloth, and so the dyestuff industry developed. Today, dyes are made for cloth, leather, paper, paints, and varnishes.

The pharmaceutical industry is very capital-intensive. Each new drug takes at least 12 years of research and testing before it can be put on the market. Roche, Novartis, Syngenta, Clariant, Givaudan, Meyhall, and Ciba are all Swiss-based pharmaceutical firms with research and processing plants in many parts of the world.

THE WATCH INDUSTRY

French refugees of the 16th century first brought skills to Switzerland that made possible the development of the watch industry. The first watchmakers' guild in Switzerland was established in the 17th century in Geneva. From there the industry spread out along the Jura mountains to Schaffhausen. Mass production of tiny parts began in Switzerland in 1845, long before other countries had the technology, so Switzerland gained an enormous advantage over other watchmaking areas. Every year 90 percent of the watch industry's production is exported all over the world, generating an average annual revenue of 10 billion Swiss francs (US$8 billion).

In 1921 the Swiss Laboratory of Horological Research was set up so Swiss manufacturers could pool ideas. In 1967 the first quartz watch was manufactured in Switzerland. Liquid crystal displays (LCDs), electrochromic displays, combined analog and digital displays, and optic sensors were all developed in Switzerland. The most recent inventions are a watch that is 0.98 mm thick and a human voice-responsive watch.

After the 1970s, the whole industry was reorganized to meet the increasing competition from Japan's inexpensive quartz watches. Switzerland has learned to compete effectively in this area, where price is an important factor. However, it still dominates the world markets in expensive watches with handmade mechanical parts.

TEXTILES

Fabric and lace are two of the oldest manufactured goods in Switzerland. The textile industry dates back to the Middle Ages when spinning and weaving were the dominant professions in certain towns. Silk was associated with Zürich, drapery with Fribourg, and linen and cotton with Saint Gall. These were cottage industries, with small home workshops producing materials for the towns' buyers. Even now, textile companies are small compared to other industries and are still decentralized.

The textile industry relies on a good export market and is susceptible to economic downturns in other countries. After World War II, for example, the embroidery industry, which had employed 100,000 people in the northeastern cantons, was virtually wiped out. But the industry has regained some of its former strength. In 2002 textile industry exports were worth 2.2 billion Swiss francs (US$1.8 billion). Export destinations are mainly Germany, Italy, France, Austria, and the United States.

Above: A wool-processing plant in operation. The textile industry is the oldest in Switzerland. Automation has led to restructuring, and today Switzerland is one of the main exporters of machinery and equipment for the textile industry.

Opposite, top and bottom: A Swiss watch factory, and Swatch watches on display. Switzerland's watch industry produces everything from chronometers to quartz and mechanical watches—all with the same Swiss precision and accuracy.

TOURISM

Switzerland has been a magnet for tourists since the 18th century, when geologist Horace Saussure published an ode to the Alps, praising their beauty. Switzerland has clean air, beautiful scenery, winter and other sports, lots of history, and plenty of culture. More than 11 million foreign tourists visit the country every year.

Tourism employs one of the largest workforces in the country. In 2001 Switzerland earned 22.4 billion Swiss francs (US$18 billion) from tourism, making it the third biggest earner after machinery and chemicals.

Unlike in other countries in Western Europe, in Switzerland tourism is not limited to the summer season. Winter offers activities such as skiing, sledding, tobogganing, and ice-skating, while summer brings golf, boating, walking, and climbing. The major winter resorts are Saint-Moritz, Gstaad, Interlaken, Chambéry, Davos, and Zermatt.

Tourism has had a beneficial effect on the country in ways other than national income. Regions that might have become depopulated have developed as tourist areas; chalets and cottages that might have fallen into ruin have become holiday homes.

But there are drawbacks. Demand for new ski resorts and hotels have made claims on an already shrinking countryside. Laws have been introduced to control the design of the new resorts and to protect endangered species. Visitors are now encouraged to visit during the less busy seasons—spring and fall.

Switzerland's scenic landscape and excellent tourist facilities make it an ideal vacation spot throughout the year. Resort chalets such as this cater to the many tourists who vacation in Switzerland annually, including a large number of Swiss.

BANKING

Perhaps Switzerland's most famous industry is banking. The idea of saving for the future is deeply rooted in Swiss society and has given rise to a unique financial network. Many foreign investors use Swiss banks, attracted by laws regarding secrecy and the stability of Swiss society. Investors can make use of numbered bank accounts, whose ownership is known only to a few people. However, if criminal activity is suspected, the bank's respect for the secrecy of its client can be dismissed. The net profit of all Swiss banks in 2003 was 12.9 billion Swiss francs (US$10.4 billion). Union de Banques Suisses (UBS), the largest Swiss bank and the world's largest asset manager, made a profit of 6.4 billion Swiss francs (US$5.1 billion) in the same year.

Information on stocks and bonds is monitored on the floor of the Zürich Stock Exchange via an efficient computer network system.

FOREIGN WORKERS

For many years the rate of increase of the Swiss population has not kept up with the needs of industry and so workers from other countries, chiefly neighboring European ones, have come to live in the country. Apart from expatriates, there are also guest workers from Italy, Spain, and Portugal. They provide the low-paid manual labor needed to construct some of Switzerland's major infrastructure projects, such as highways.

Switzerland has benefited a great deal in the past from the influx of foreign workers and refugees from European wars. The official figures for foreign workers are actually lower than the real ones since there are many people living near the Swiss borders who commute into Switzerland for work. Many seasonal workers, too, move to tourist areas such as Lugano just for one season before returning to Italy or Spain.

ENVIRONMENT

CHARACTERISTICS OF SWITZERLAND'S geography and economy make sound environmental practices desirable. A landlocked country with limited resources, Switzerland nevertheless boasts a major tourist industry that draws visitors enraptured by its beautiful lakes, breathtaking mountains, and skiing facilities. All these factors, taken together, make the Swiss a people deeply committed to environmental protection.

In many regards, Switzerland is perhaps the "greenest" country in the industrialized world. The Swiss have long taken a commendably active stance in support of the environment and against pollution. The country is a signatory and/or active participant in almost all the major international antipollution and environmental treaties and agreements, such as the Kyoto Protocol on reduction of greenhouse gases and the Law of the Sea Treaty (even if Switzerland is an entirely landlocked country).

One clear measure of the Swiss concern for the environment is the strength of the national Greens Party. Founded in 1971, the Greens have since grown to become the fifth-largest party in Switzerland, where a large number of small parties dot the political landscape. Today the Swiss Greens Party is the largest party outside of the governing coalition of four small parties. Its growth peaked in the 1990s when Greens Party members held prominent political positions, such as Verena Diener, who was president of the Zürich state government in 1999–2000.

For the most part, big environmental programs in Switzerland are coordinated and overseen by an official agency known as BUWAL, which is a German acronym for the Swiss Federal Agency for the Environment, Forests, and Landscape.

Above: **The Staubbach Falls plunge nearly 1,000 feet (305 m) over a vertical rock face in Lauterbrunnen Valley in the Bernese Alps, Bern.**

Opposite: **A cow grazes at the foot of a mountain in western Switzerland.**

Polyethylene tereph-thalate (PET) plastic is highly recyclable. With more than 12,000 collection points across the country, Switzerland recycled 72 percent of all the PET plastic that was sold there in 2002.

RECYCLING

As with many of their Western European neighbors, the Swiss are actively engaged in a variety of recycling programs, most of them run or supported by the federal or local governments.

There is a trash separation program for household hazardous waste, and on the streets there are huge containers to collect used glass, paper, and other items for recycling. In addition, metals, plastics, and old shoes and clothing are recycled. About 91 percent of all aluminum cans are recycled, as are 70 percent of pet food cans and 40 percent of aluminum tubing. Up to 40,000 tons of old shoes and clothing are collected and recycled annually. The Swiss also have take-back recycling systems for office equipment, domestic appliances, and consumer electronics. Under this system, mandated by law, stores that sell these appliances are required to take them back from their customers when they no longer function. The stores then see that these appliances are either recycled or disposed of safely.

As a result of these programs, Switzerland manages to recycle half of all its household waste. Annual garbage production in Switzerland amounts to just 880 pounds (399 kg) per capita, or half the amount the average American throws away.

WASTE INCINERATION

Swiss authorities usually employ economic incentives to promote responsible waste management, and most solid waste in Europe is incinerated rather than put into landfills. In one successful program to further reduce the country's dependence on foreign energy sources, Switzerland barred burnable waste from all its landfills in the year 2000. This waste is sent to municipal incinerators and used to produce electricity and low-cost steam heat for public buildings in Switzerland. This program is beneficial to the industry as the incinerators now offer a market for the companies' burnable waste.

However, 1 percent of all waste in Switzerland is burned illegally, generating 1,000 times the amount of dioxins produced by municipal incinerators and making up 41 percent of all toxic emissions in the country. But even here, the Swiss set a standard for environmental protection—environmental violators are actively pursued by the authorities.

Swiss authorities and businesses are taking steps to cut back significantly on forms of harmful pollution, such as vehicle emissions. This small, environmentally friendly Smart car was a joint venture of the Swiss Swatch company and the German automobile manufacturer, Mercedes.

ECHETS TOXIQUES ZONE
CONTAMINEE
GIFTMÜLL
GEFAHRENZONE
OXIC WASTE DANGER ZONE

GREENPEACE   GREENPEACE   GREENPEACE

Greenpeace activists block access to a toxic waste dump in Bonfol near the French border. These activists demand that chemical companies clean up the site. The disused landfill holds around 114,000 tons of waste, which was dumped there between 1961 and 1976, mainly by chemical companies based in Basel.

THE DARK SIDE

In addition to open-air burning, the Swiss face problems with air pollution from vehicle emissions. They also suffer the effects of acid rain, some of which travels in uninvited from their neighbors. Further, there is a disturbing loss of biodiversity.

One major problem involves pollution of the land. For example, in 2002 a government report revealed that there were over 50,000 polluted sites in Switzerland, with 3,000 of them representing significant risks and requiring remedial action.

Cleaning up this pollution will be costly, but the Swiss government is committed to the project. Some sites only need to be sealed off from the public and left to decontaminate over time. However, in some cases it will be necessary to decontaminate the sites as quickly as is safely possible. The Swiss government expects to spend 5 billion Swiss francs (US$4 billion) to accomplish its goals, although the Swiss branch of the environmental group Greenpeace contends that the cost of a thorough clean-up of all present hazardous sites in Switzerland could actually cost up to 10 times that amount.

While environmental activists and some Swiss officials blame Switzerland's massive chemical industry for the pollution, pastoral industries also contribute a significant share to the Swiss pollution woes. For instance, pesticides alone pollute half of the groundwater in Switzerland. Fertilizers also pollute. The significance of the Swiss agricultural industry and the Swiss desire to protect and help its farmers make this area of environmental clean-up a special challenge.

BIODIVERSITY

Another area where Switzerland gets less than the highest marks is in the preservation of its biodiversity. Switzerland is thought to be a pristine land welcoming to all life forms, but, in fact, 224 species of plants and animals have become extinct in the country over the last 150 years. Today Switzerland maintains a Red List of endangered plants and animals for special protection. The causes for a loss of biodiversity include the rerouting of water, drying up of wetlands, building and road construction, destruction of natural habitats, and intensive land cultivation. Government agencies are focused on biodiversity monitoring and conservation programs.

Four lion cubs scale a log on their first outdoor trip in a zoo in southern Switzerland. The country has a number of endangered animals, such as the aquatic warbler, common sturgeon, and European otter.

Mountain climbers are silhouetted against the sky as they walk on top of the Rhône glacier in the Swiss Alps. The glacier is the source of the river Rhône, which runs into Lake Geneva and from there to France.

MOST IMPORTANT SWISS NATURAL RESOURCE

Energy conservation is a major concern for the Swiss, who have no oil reserves of their own and almost no coal or other fossil fuels. In fact, fossil fuels produce just 1.3 percent of Swiss electricity. However, thanks to the abundance of powerful rivers and the dams that have been built to harness them, Switzerland produces large amounts of hydroelectric power. Renewable and abundant, water power is often called Switzerland's most important natural resource.

Water power produces almost 60 percent of Switzerland's electricity, in the form of hydroelectric power. In addition, because of this valuable resource, Switzerland exports electricity to many of its European neighbors.

The sources of hydroelectric power in Switzerland are two of Europe's largest rivers, the Rhine and the Rhône, which begin in the Alps and run from there through Switzerland to neighboring countries. Furthermore, Switzerland's rugged, mountainous topography and high levels of precipitation create suitable conditions for a first-rate hydroelectric industry.

Interestingly, most of the country's hydroelectric power is produced in just four cantons: Uri, Valais, Ticino, and Graubünden. This energy is produced with the use of large dams built in the Alps, along with smaller dams constructed on the Swiss rivers. Two of Europe's highest dams, the Mauvoisin and Grande Dixence, are in the canton of Valais.

Studies indicate that 80 to 90 percent of the country's hydroelectric potential has already been tapped. But despite the ever-increasing demands for electricity, it is deemed unlikely that the remaining 10 to 20 percent of

The Mauvoisin Dam in Valais is one of the highest dams in Europe at 777 feet (237 m).

that potential will be exploited. This is because further development of this relatively clean, renewable, and environmentally friendly power could itself do significant, perhaps irreparable, environmental damage.

While there are quite a number of areas where new and large Alpine dams could be constructed to deliver large amounts of energy, these sites lie in fragile environments. Large dam projects would almost certainly upset the delicate balance and ruin the natural beauty of these areas. This would damage another major Swiss industry, tourism, which brings in revenue from visitors and provides employment to the Swiss.

Swiss energy experts do see some excellent potential for further hydroelectric power development in the country's many rivers but caution that these new facilities could provide only a small increase over present output levels.

THE SWISS

PEOPLE OF DIFFERENT ETHNIC origins and languages, the Swiss have found a unique way to coexist and maintain their diversity. Switzerland's federalism incorporates an enormous respect for the cultural differences of its people and a determination to preserve those differences. If a nation can be said to have certain characteristics, the Swiss are conservative, unfussy, prudent, and industrious.

Switzerland stands at a geographical crossroads where several cultures meet. Switzerland also has religious diversity. Catholics and Protestants live side by side in almost equal numbers. There are also tiny Greek Orthodox and Jewish communities and a growing Muslim population.

Switzerland has a population of about 7.4 million. In 2003 there were approximately 809,000 foreign workers in the country.

Left: **Two Swiss men engage in conversation.**

Opposite: **A girl displays fingernails painted with the colors of the Swiss national flag during a Swiss National Day celebration.**

THE PEOPLE OF TICINO

Ticino is the part of Switzerland that is closest to Italy. At various times in Switzerland's history it was annexed by Italy. Most of its people speak Italian and are more Mediterranean in look and character.

Ticino is a mountainous canton and historically has been depressed economically. Farmers grew grapes, tobacco, olives, and vegetables to survive. It is the warmest part of Switzerland in the summer, when there are severe thunderstorms that cause the Ticino River to flood much of the arable land. Winters, however, are relatively mild. The typical Ticino house is a stone-roofed cottage high in the hills. Lakes Maggiore and Lugano occupy a considerable area of the canton. The scenic lakes, mountainous areas, and mild climate fostered a tourism industry after the end of World War II.

This tourism and the increasing wealth of the other cantons have affected the lifestyle of the Ticino people. Many of the old stone-roofed cottages in the mountains have been purchased as summer homes for wealthy Zürich residents. This has increased the local real estate value, often to the dissatisfaction of the residents. In addition many of the local inhabitants have emigrated to the other more prosperous cantons to work.

There have been improvements in the lives of the people who have chosen to stay. Although agriculture is still practiced, Ticino has become a center of tourism and international finance. In the city of Lugano, many people have found work in the service industries.

THE PEOPLE OF GRAUBÜNDEN

The origin of the people who live in this upland region of Switzerland can be traced to the Rhaetians, an ancient people related to the Etruscans in Italy. Thus the people living in Graubünden (or Grisons, in French) are of a completely different origin than the Swiss of French and German heritage, and their language has evolved from different sources.

Most Europeans are believed to be of Indo-European origin, but not so the people of Graubünden. The Romansh languages have Etruscan, Semitic, and perhaps Celtic

influences on top of the basic Latin imposed by the Romans. Although Graubünden also contains Swiss-German and Italian speakers today, the Romansh language is spoken by about a third of the population. Graubünden is the only official trilingual Swiss canton.

Graubünden is Switzerland's largest canton, occupying about 2,743 square miles (7,106 square km) in the southeastern part of the country. The canton got its name from the Gray League (Grauer Bund), which was formed in 1395 with the purpose of restoring peace to the area. The league was so named because most of the members, who were peasants, wore gray clothes.

Graubünden is largely rural. The people practice pastoral agriculture and produce wine, and many of them find employment in the very exclusive winter resorts in the area. Graubünden is also the home of the Swiss National Park, the only national park in Switzerland.

Above: **Horse-drawn sleighs provide a means of transportation for the people of Graubünden, which is one of Switzerland's most picturesque spots and is an important tourist destination. The tourist industry provides jobs for many of the canton's inhabitants.**

Opposite: **A family vineyard near Mendrisio in the southern canton of Ticino. Wine is produced in large quantities in the vineyards of this region.**

THE PEOPLE OF THE VALAIS

The Valais was a late entrant into the Confederation, joining in 1815 after centuries of exploitation by the French dukes of Savoy and eventually Napoleon's France. For Valais, joining the Confederation was a last resort rather than an achievement.

The Valais is a narrow valley 93 miles (150 km) long, lying between the Valaisian and Bernese alps, and the skyline is dominated by mountains. Extending from the central valley are many smaller valleys that even today are quite inaccessible.

The people of the Valais have always seen themselves as a race apart from the rest of the Swiss. If a whole group of people can be characterized, they would probably describe themselves as headstrong, self-confident, and very independent. They are largely French-speaking and have a very distinctive accent that any Swiss can recognize after hearing the first few words. In some rural areas a dialect of French is spoken.

The Matterhorn and the resort town of Zermatt attract tourists. Wine production and cattle breeding are still practiced. Each spring the animals are taken to the summer pastures on the mountains and brought down again in the fall.

IMMIGRANTS

For centuries foreigners have come to Switzerland as a place of refuge. Some very famous people have made Switzerland their home, however temporarily. The 19th-century German writers Johann Wolfgang von Goethe and Friedrich von Schiller lived in Switzerland for a time, and Mary Shelley wrote her novel *Frankenstein* in Switzerland. Richard Wagner, the German composer, left his native Germany and took refuge in Switzerland. Friedrich Nietzsche, who taught at Basel University, got the idea for his work *Thus Spake Zarathustra* while on vacation in Engadine, in Graubünden. German-born Albert Einstein became a Swiss citizen in 1901 and was working in the patent office in Bern when he developed his famous theory of relativity. The great Russian writer Fyodor Dostoyevsky also lived in Switzerland. Russian revolutionaries Vladimir Lenin, Grigory Zinovyev, and Leon Trotsky, Russian composer Igor Stravinsky, and Irish writer James Joyce all waited out at least part of World War I in Switzerland. Joyce spent his final days in Zürich.

Many famous people still find their way to Switzerland, attracted by the banking system and the tax concessions. Wealthy immigrants have also chosen to live in Switzerland because of its stability and high quality of life. There are foreign workers attracted by the good wages, and those who escape from difficult political situations in their home countries.

There are roughly 1.5 million foreigners living in Switzerland, making up 20 percent of the population. The statistics do not include seasonal workers and people living near the Swiss border who commute daily into the country to work. A significant number of political refugees and expatriates have also added to the total number of foreigners. Approximately 37,000 immigrants from various countries received their Swiss citizenship in 2003.

EMIGRANTS

When Switzerland industrialized, many people chose to leave the country in search of a new agricultural life rather than make the move to the cities to work. The United States and Australia were major destinations for poor Swiss farmers.

In the more distant past, the Swiss left to work as mercenaries in foreign armies. Today the majority of Swiss who leave are professionals going abroad for the experience or to promote some Swiss industry. In 2004 there were approximately 600,000 Swiss living abroad. The largest Swiss expatriate community can be found in France, where 158,000 Swiss live. There are 70,000 Swiss living in the United States.

Swiss living abroad retain their right to vote in elections but many do not exercise their voting rights. For example, only 18 percent of Swiss expatriates took part in a November 2002 vote on an asylum initiative. The

initiative sought to ascertain the age, origin, and identity of asylum seekers from certain countries when they had first arrived at reception centers in Switzerland. This was to filter out people suspected of criminal activities and to prevent abuse of the asylum system.

COSTUMES

There are almost as many different traditional costumes in Switzerland as there are valleys. These costumes, highly regarded and valued, are worn during the many festive occasions in Switzerland. Many costumes display the Swiss craft of embroidery. The most distinctive ones are probably those of the Gruyère region. The *armailli* (arm-ah-EE-yee), or herdsman, of the Gruyère wears the

bredzon (bredd-ZAHNN), a short blue cloth or canvas jacket with sleeves gathered at the shoulders, and edelweiss embroidered on the lapels. The woman's dress from the same region is plain and worn with a red scarf round the neck. For festivals, a silk apron and a long-sleeved jacket are added. The straw hat is edged with velvet and has crocheted ribbons hanging off it.

Women from Saint Gall wear shimmering gold lace caps, while women from Appenzell wear lace caps with spreading wings. The Appenzell herdsman wears intricate trousers with heavily patterned straps, and suspenders carrying pictures of the cows he tends. He also wears a silver earring on his right ear. In Nidwalden and Obwalden, the woman's dress is ornamented with silver, and a silver comb is worn in the side of the hair. The man's shirt from the same region is heavily embroidered.

Above: **Two Swiss women pose in their elaborately ornamented traditional costumes in Zürich.**

Opposite top: **A signboard depicts the traditional dress of the herdsman of the Gruyère region.**

Opposite bottom: **An Appenzell herdsman's hat is decorated with flowers.**

LIFESTYLE

SWITZERLAND ENJOYS A PRIVILEGED POSITION in the world. This is due, among other things, to its early industrialization and a well-educated population that has enabled the country to specialize in producing high-quality products and providing valuable services, such as banking and investing.

The population consists of people from diverse ethnic and linguistic groups, and the nation has learned to survive as a cohesive unit.

There is no doubt that the Swiss are conscious of both their own wealth and their exemption from the world's major upheavals. More than just a collection of bank managers, clockmakers, and chocolate entrepreneurs, Switzerland has led the world in other important ways, such as in its long tradition of aid and disaster relief work.

Left: A wooden farmhouse in Switzerland offers a picturesque and tranquil scene. Here, a Swiss mother takes time off from her chores to play with her child.

Opposite: Pedestrians cross a street in Geneva.

LIFE IN THE CITIES

The cities and towns of Switzerland are home to 68 percent of the population. Each city has its own character, determined by its population mix, its focus as a city, and its architectural heritage. As in other world cities, urban growth and the demand for office buildings in the inner city have meant that large residential areas have grown around the cities. Swiss cities are heavily populated, and commuters on their way to work may spend time waiting in line for buses, streetcars, or a ferryboat.

In the cities, sidewalk cafés are one of the focal points of daily life. In summer, they are crowded with workers and tourists having their lunch or watching the world go by. In the French-speaking cities, the people prefer to drink wine with their lunch, while in the German-speaking towns, such as Zürich, beer rivals wine as the popular drink.

Commuters at a Zürich streetcar station.

Nightlife in the cities begins early, at around 8 P.M. For those who want a night out there is sufficient entertainment to keep them occupied, from restaurants and movie theaters to clubs and bars. The evening's activities end early. By midnight, the restaurants and bars are closed and only the most avant-garde of clubs stay open until 2 or 3 A.M.

In Zürich and other major cities, drugs are a real problem, with some city parks becoming centers for young drug users who have dropped out of mainstream society. Many cantons give free syringes to drug users in an attempt to combat AIDS. Increasingly, Swiss cities are experiencing the mugging and petty theft that accompany a drug culture.

Switzerland has flirted with the idea of joining the European Union on and off for some years now. The urban Swiss realize their future lies as part of a united Europe but fear that their centuries-long neutrality and decentralized democracy will be at stake if they join the European Union.

Sidewalk cafés are frequented by Swiss and tourists, who enjoy the alfresco atmosphere.

LIFE IN THE COUNTRY

Around 32 percent of the population of Switzerland live in rural areas, but only about 5 percent are actually engaged in agriculture. Over the last century, the urbanization of the country has seen large population movements from the countryside into the cities. At the same time, agricultural output has increased by means of mechanization, improved fertilizers, and economies of scale as farms get much larger.

People in the rural cantons of Switzerland have historically been more conservative in their outlook than those living in the cities. Now many of them find work in the tourism industry, which in Switzerland employs them more or less all year round. Their work day is determined by the same work ethic employed in cities. Hotels must be cleaned and the guests catered to, restaurants must provide the tourists with meals, and sports centers and health spas must be kept in efficient running condition.

A farmer enlists the help of his family on their farm in Vaud. As more and more farm workers choose other occupations, farming has become increasingly mechanized.

For the 5 percent of Swiss still engaged in farming, life could undergo a drastic change if Switzerland should one day join the European Union. The country has long protected its farmers from foreign competition, but if it became an EU member, it would have to drop all tariffs and other restrictions against agricultural products from other EU members. In addition, the subsidies for Swiss farms in the form of fixed prices would be decided in Brussels (the EU capital),

not Bern. This is just one more important factor that makes the Swiss reluctant to join the European Union.

In Alpine regions such as the Valais, people live in tiny communities that are continually shrinking. As more young people emigrate to the cities, life becomes harder for those left behind, especially since tourism and the desire for country homes has put the price of houses in the countryside out of reach for any poorer person who wishes to live there. The large number of vacation homes also ensures that the winter months are lonely ones for those who live in the countryside all year round. Spring and summer, however, bring lots of visitors and festivals to liven up their days.

Guarda, a village in the Engadine of Graubünden. Many village homes such as these have been purchased as summer residences by wealthy, urban Swiss.

LIFE'S MAJOR EVENTS

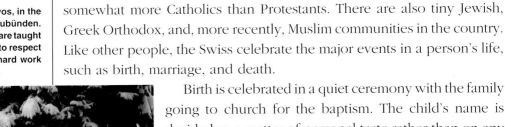

The vast majority of the people in Switzerland are Christians, with somewhat more Catholics than Protestants. There are also tiny Jewish, Greek Orthodox, and, more recently, Muslim communities in the country. Like other people, the Swiss celebrate the major events in a person's life, such as birth, marriage, and death.

Birth is celebrated in a quiet ceremony with the family going to church for the baptism. The child's name is decided as a matter of personal taste rather than on any religious grounds. In church, the child is given godparents, who promise to be responsible for the child's religious upbringing. In most cases this is symbolic, although the parents usually choose a close family member or friend.

At age 7, the Catholic child receives instruction on the meaning of Holy Communion, and then in a public ceremony receives the Host with other children of the same age. At age 13, both Protestant and Catholic children are confirmed in their religion. Catholic children take an additional Confirmation name at this ceremony, although it is rarely used.

Marriage is still popular in Switzerland, although there are many young people who choose not to observe this ceremony. A church wedding is often followed by a honeymoon abroad. Nowadays many people marry in a civil ceremony.

Swiss funerals are quiet affairs. The family attends a funeral service in church, followed by the burial in the local graveyard.

Children in Davos, in the canton of Graubünden. Swiss children are taught at an early age to respect the virtues of hard work and enterprise.

Besides these major events in life, the Swiss observe other cycles. The change in seasons is celebrated each year, especially in rural areas such as the Valais. There, the farmers wait for spring to come so that they can go with the animals to the high pastures, gradually working their way back down the mountain as the grass is eaten. Celebrations take place during this period, with festivals and mock battles between the cows.

The events of the Christian year are also celebrated in much the same way as in other Christian countries. Religious celebrations, both somber and joyous, are observed in accordance with the Christian calendar, the most important ones being Christmas, Easter, and Corpus Christi.

A well-tended Swiss cemetery. The majority of the Swiss population are either Roman Catholics or Protestants.

A Swiss family gets together for a meal. The Swiss have strong family ties and often go on social outings together.

SOCIAL INTERACTION

The Swiss are great consumers of the media. Most cities are connected to cable television and so there are many programs to watch. The Swiss are also avid newspaper readers. Swiss social life revolves around these things and the family. Nightlife, as we have seen, ends early. People work fairly hard—the average work week is 41.7 hours—and at the end of a long day, most people go home to their families. The coffee shops and bars in the cities and villages are meeting places where people can discuss politics or just read their newspapers in companionable silence.

In a society made up of four distinct language groups, at least three religious groups, and many foreigners, the ability to get along with one's neighbors is a desirable quality that has been bred into the Swiss as a way of life. The Swiss are essentially home-loving, careful people, with a high degree of tolerance, great interest in preserving their cultural heritage, and a great sense of civic duty. They appreciate the benefits of their country's neutrality and the wealth that a public-spirited workforce can bring. There are very few strikes among workers in Switzerland. The Swiss have learned that all differences can be negotiated rather than fought out in public. Since 1937 there has been a regularly renewed agreement between employers and workers to settle their disputes peacefully.

THE ROLE OF WOMEN

Switzerland is by its own admission a conservative country. In a country that values democracy so highly, it is strange that women did not get the right to vote in federal elections until 1971. One demicanton, Appenzell Inner Rhodes, denied women this right for almost 20 more years, with various referenda to change the law failing. Finally, in 1991 the Swiss high court ordered Appenzell Inner Rhodes to join the rest of Switzerland and allow women the right to vote.

On paper, women have had the right to equal pay since 1981, although they are still underrepresented in many areas, particularly in politics. In fact, an official study early this century found that women in Switzerland generally earn 21.5 percent less than their male counterparts, although this earnings gap had been shrinking throughout the previous decade.

In 1984 Elisabeth Kopp became the first woman to be elected to the seven-person Federal Council, but she resigned before her term of office ended over a political scandal of which she was later cleared. Trade union leader Christiane Brunner campaigned for a seat on the Federal Council in 1993 but was denied after she had a smear campaign directed against her. Ruth Dreifuss was the second woman to be elected to the Federal Council in 1993 and became Switzerland's first female president in 1999. Another woman, Ruth Metzler, gained a seat in the Federal Council in 1999. Metzler's entry into the Council was notable not only because of her gender but also because of her youth. She was only 34 years old at the time of her appointment. In parliament, women occupy only 24 percent of the seats in the lower house and 15 percent in the upper house.

Two women walking in the hills near Zermatt, a town famous for its proximity to the Matterhorn. Swiss women obtained the right to vote in 1971.

There are eight universities in Switzerland, four of them in French-speaking areas and four in German-speaking areas. The universities are paid for by the cantons, with the aid of government subsidies.

SOCIAL STRUCTURES

Switzerland is a welfare state, meaning that as part of its duties the state provides all its citizens with generously subsidized health care, pensions, maternity benefits, and education. These benefits are paid for on the federal level using money that workers contribute to a compulsory national insurance fund; they can draw on this fund in their old age or when sick. At the cantonal level, each canton provides funds and services to the destitute or needy. At the commune level, additional funds are allowed for individual needs. This explains why every Swiss resident must be a member of a commune and remains a member of that commune unless he or she applies to join another. It is ultimately the responsibility of the commune to look after its needy.

EDUCATION

In Switzerland, each canton is responsible for drawing up its own curriculum, school materials, and teacher-training program for primary, middle, and advanced school education. There are 26 different educational systems operating in Switzerland, one in each canton. The cantons must meet federal standards, but beyond that each canton is autonomous.

Federal regulations determine that children start school at age 6 or 7 and continue for eight years. In some cantons, an optional ninth year has been introduced, and all the cantons offer two optional preschool years of kindergarten. Most children attend preschool for one or two years at age 5 or 6. After that, there are between four to six years of primary school, depending on the canton, and three to five years of secondary school. Thus in some cantons, children go to secondary school at age 10, while in others, they move to secondary school at age 12.

At the secondary level, children are streamed; that is, they are put into different schools depending on their ability. One category of secondary school offers four years of apprenticeship training leading to a craft or trade of some kind; another offers academic education, where children are prepared for university or an institute of technology; while the third offers vocational training, which is conducted in collaboration with private companies. Each canton arranges the training of apprentices. Students study part-time and spend a large proportion of their day in the workplace learning their trade. Higher vocational training in colleges trains students to become engineers, managers, economists, or social workers.

The Swiss education system has its drawbacks, since at the time they enter secondary school children are still young and either do not always know what they want or have not yet reached their full potential. The system is being reviewed so that streaming is delayed, to give young people more time to develop and gain a well-rounded education.

A classroom lesson in progress. The literacy rate in Switzerland is virtually 100 percent.

Swiss soldiers guard the entrance of an embassy in Bern.

NATIONAL DEFENSE

For a neutral country, Switzerland spends a great deal of money on national defense—around the same amount it spends on social welfare.

Switzerland has 120,000 full-time professional soldiers, and the state considers that each man's military obligation is just as important as his civic ones. Thus part of every Swiss man's life is devoted to his military duties.

At age 20, all Swiss men are required to attend a 17-week training session where they learn the basics and are given their equipment. This equipment, including weapons, ammunition, gas mask, and uniform, is kept at home and soldiers are responsible for maintaining it. Between ages 20 and 32, men attend eight three-week retraining courses. Between ages 33 and 42, they are put in the military reserve and attend three two-week courses. After age 43 and until age 50, they are still reserve soldiers but are only required to perform one week of training per year. In total, military training takes up about a year and a half of a man's life, more for officers. Women may volunteer for military training.

Switzerland's total military manpower ability is 1.9 million. In 2001 the country's military expenditure was $2.5 billion. The country has tanks, jet fighters, canons, and missiles. In addition, there are camouflaged underground storage caverns and military bases, all of them designed to withstand nuclear blasts.

Other underground storage spaces hold medicine, repair shops for military machinery, and food. For the civilians, there are also underground shelters capable of withstanding heavy bombing. In the early 1970s a

THE RED CROSS

If Switzerland has not taken sides in any major European war in the last 400 or 500 years, it has also not turned its back on the suffering of those engaged in those wars. It has become part of the lifestyle of the Swiss, and perhaps part of the justification for their neutrality, to look after those in need. Switzerland is the home and birthplace of the International Red Cross. It was an eccentric Swiss who started the Swiss movement to set up the organization.

Jean-Henri Dunant (1828–1910) had no intention of being a world benefactor. He was as interested as any other Swiss in setting up a business for himself, and to that end he went to Algeria, where he began to trade in grain. But things went wrong. The money he borrowed in Switzerland to start his operation could not be repaid, and so he decided to enlist help from Napoleon III. He followed Napoleon to the Battle of Solferino (1859), where he accidentally witnessed the terrible casualties that the battle caused. He spent two days personally helping the injured and then returned to Switzerland with a lot more on his mind than grain. He toured Switzerland talking about what he had witnessed, and his actions brought about the signing of the first Geneva Convention. Dunant became a public hero for a while, until his creditors caught up with him and he went into hiding, living in poverty in a country village. He got his reward when he received the Nobel Peace Prize in 1901—the very first one. Today, the headquarters of the International Red Cross *(above)* is situated in Geneva and is staffed by Swiss citizens. Switzerland is the guardian of the four Geneva Conventions regarding prisoners of war, the wounded, and refugees.

government-mandated program to provide people with bomb shelters was inaugurated. Today Switzerland boasts pretty close to a readily available place in a shelter for every resident. These bomb shelters have steel-reinforced concrete walls and armored doors.

The original law required every new building to include a bomb shelter, although with the end of the Cold War, the Swiss government loosened this requirement somewhat.

RELIGION

CHRISTIANITY FIRST CAME to Switzerland through the Roman merchants and soldiers, but it was not until the early Middle Ages, in the seventh century and quite late in the history of Christianity, that the bulk of the Swiss population was converted. This final conversion was due to the work of a group of traveling missionaries, led by Saint Columban and Saint Gall or Gallus, two dedicated and devout Irish monks. They found an ancient Celtic religion in Switzerland and hurled into the lakes the graven images of the pagan religion.

In the 16th century, Catholic Switzerland was racked by the Reformation, when the new Protestants tried to take political power in Zürich. This led to war between the Protestant and the Catholic states. Switzerland, like the rest of Europe, was divided along religious lines.

Those divisions again became inflamed in the 19th century, when Lucerne, a predominantly Catholic canton, decided to put its school system under the control of the Jesuits. Protestant groups attacked the city, and the seven Catholic cantons decided to secede from the Confederation. The Sonderbund civil war followed. The dispute led to the Swiss Constitution of 1848, which among other things, declared complete religious tolerance, with the exception of the Jesuits, who were banned from Switzerland. This ban was officially lifted only in 1973.

Above: **A village church in Gsteig, in southwestern Switzerland.**

Opposite: **The twin towers of the Grossmünster church are a distinctive landmark in Zürich.**

77

The 1874 Constitution guaranteed full religious liberty but repeated the 1848 Constitution's prohibition of settlement by Jesuits and their affiliated societies in Switzerland. This anti-Jesuit article was repealed in a national referendum in 1973.

The importance of religious tolerance has remained to this day. The once clear divisions of cantons into Catholic and Protestant camps has softened since the Industrial Revolution, when large numbers of people from the rural cantons moved to the cities. Now the Catholic areas are mainly the southern Italian-speaking ones as well as those in central Switzerland. The French-speaking areas, and the areas to the north and east, are largely Protestant. Nationally, roughly 46 percent are Catholics, while 40 percent are Protestant. Muslims, Jews, and people of other faiths make up 5 percent, while the nonaffiliated make up close to 9 percent of the residents of Switzerland.

PROTESTANTISM

During the Reformation, the two main centers of Protestantism in Switzerland were Zürich, under the influence of Huldrych Zwingli, and Geneva, under the influence of John Calvin. Zürich was and is mostly German-speaking; Geneva largely French-speaking. Later, Vaud, the canton north of Geneva, and Neuchâtel, its neighbor, were converted. Bern, the largest canton in central Switzerland, also joined the Reformation. As time passed and the citizens of the cantons moved about within the Federation, each city developed a character of its own but had a mixed community of Protestants and Catholics. The numerous Protestant groups formed the Federation of Swiss Evangelical Churches.

In its early stages, Protestantism in Switzerland was a fiercely puritan religion, disapproving of all frivolity and excess. This can still be seen in the Protestant churches of Switzerland, which are simple, austere, and bare compared to the Catholic churches with their highly elaborate artwork, decoration, and artifacts.

Calvinism, the basis of modern Swiss Protestantism, began as a rejection of some of the tenets of the Church of Rome. It rejected the role of the Pope as God's representative and instead declared that all people could petition directly to God. It refused to accept any doctrine beyond those laid down in the Bible, so that the belief in transubstantiation (the changing of the bread and wine into the body and blood of Christ) was rejected. The ornate decoration of the older churches was thrown out, as was much of the ceremony. More importantly, perhaps, Calvinists believed in predestination—the idea that a soul's eventual destiny, especially its place in heaven or hell, is foreordained by God.

Today, Protestant churches are managed in each canton by a synod, a body of lay persons who decide on church matters. Swiss Protestants celebrate the same religious events as Catholics. Christmas, Easter, and Lent figure largely in their religious calendar and are celebrated in very similar ways.

After the Swiss converted to Christianity in the early Middle Ages, Roman Catholics and Protestants waged fierce religious wars in the 16th and 17th centuries. Together, these two groups still account for the majority of the population, although they now live in harmony.

ROMAN CATHOLICISM

Roman Catholics form almost half the population of Switzerland. During the Reformation, the rural cantons and the cantons in central Switzerland were not affected by the new ideas of Calvin and Zwingli. Those states now make up the predominantly Catholic areas.

The Roman Catholic and Protestant churches in Switzerland share a belief in the same God. Their differences are in matters of doctrine and government. The chief differences between the two religions are that Catholics believe in confession and absolution, and revere Mary, the mother of Jesus, in the belief that she will intercede on behalf of the repentant, while Protestants do not accept these doctrines. The government of the Catholic Church is less democratic. Ultimate power lies with the Pope in Rome, and each diocese in a country is governed by a bishop.

Like Protestants, Roman Catholics celebrate the main events of the Christian calendar. Christmas is a public holiday in Switzerland, but for both sects it is a private family affair, with little public activity on the two days of the holiday. Catholic and Protestant children both celebrate Saint Nicholas' Day on December 6. Gifts are given, and in some areas, particularly in Graubünden, large and noisy parades take place. On Christmas Eve, Catholic families attend midnight Mass together.

Later in the year, Lent, a period of penitence and fasting, is observed, marking the 40 days that Christ spent in the wilderness. All public festivals are avoided, and people give up some luxury for the duration. On Easter Sunday, the Resurrection of Christ is celebrated.

The feast of Corpus Christi falls in late May or early June every year; it is a special celebration of the Eucharist, which has been observed since 1264. Several towns have parades, with each area stressing different themes in their costumes.

OTHER GROUPS

Besides the Roman Catholic Church, there is another Catholic diocese in Switzerland not associated with it. This is the Old Catholic Church. Differing slightly on matters of doctrine, the group is represented mostly in Bern.

Switzerland's need of foreign workers and the huge tide of refugees moving around Europe in the 1980s and 1990s has brought other religions, such as Islam, to Switzerland. Islam is now the second largest religion in the country. Muslims now make up 2 percent of the population.

There is a tiny Jewish community in the country. They represent about 0.3 percent of the population.

SAINT GALL

There has been a monastery of some sort at Saint Gallen since the traveling Irish monk Gall built a sleeping cell and a wooden church there in the seventh century. During the Middle Ages, the town of Saint Gallen became an enormously powerful ecclesiastical center. In the 18th century, the monastery and its lands were taken by the French. The monastery became a cathedral in 1847.

The Saint Gallen Cathedral *(right)* represents many different eras of architectural history, with eighth-century buildings and a Collegiate Church dating back to the 18th century. The most beautiful room in this complex of buildings is the 18th-century abbey library, with its elaborate plasterwork and paintings. It contains some very rare manuscripts, including Irish examples dating back to the period between the seventh and 12th centuries.

Leader of the Reformation in German-speaking Switzerland, Huldrych Zwingli began his work as preacher, writer, teacher, and social reformer in Glarus.

HULDRYCH ZWINGLI

Born in 1484, Zwingli was a leading figure in the Reformation. He was educated in Basel and then Bern and was ordained as a Catholic priest. He served as a chaplain with the Swiss mercenary armies in Europe and witnessed many deaths. He expressed his opposition to the mercenaries so strongly that he had to retire to the Benedictine abbey at Einsiedeln. Again he found much to criticize in the habits and behavior of the priesthood, and so came to the attention of the City Council of Zürich, which invited him to live and practice his vocation in that city.

His first sermon was electrifying. He outlined a new kind of city-state, where all the elaborate trappings and hypocrisy of the old clergy would be gone. Against the traditions of the priesthood, he married and then set about destroying all the graven images in the churches. He opposed the sale of papal indulgences, a very lucrative activity for the Church, and argued with Martin Luther over the nature of the Eucharist, refusing to accept that it might really become the body and blood of Christ. The city of Zürich went along with all his ideas, but its surrounding rural areas rejected them and a war soon followed. In the battle of Kappel (1531), he was fatally wounded and his corpse was despoiled, quartered, and burned, and his ashes scattered to the wind.

EINSIEDELN ABBEY

This Benedictine abbey in northeastern Switzerland was founded in 934 on the site of the hermitage of Saint Meinrad. Huldrych Zwingli, the religious reformer, was the parish priest from 1516 to 1518.

The abbots of the monastery were very powerful. Even when they had lost most of their power after 1789, the abbey remained a major place of pilgrimage for Europeans, who visited the Black Madonna statue. The abbey also has a library containing rare and beautiful manuscripts. To house all the pilgrims, a baroque-style church was built in the 18th century. The buildings and grounds of the church and abbey are very beautiful and remain a major tourist attraction.

John Calvin was one of the most important Protestant reformers of the 16th century. He also contributed to the Reformation in Switzerland. His ideas had a profound influence on the development of Protestantism in many parts of Europe.

JOHN CALVIN

If Zwingli's work was directed at German Zürich, then Calvin's was aimed at French Geneva. He was born in France in 1509 and educated there. By 1533 he had become a Protestant. He arrived in Geneva in 1536, when the town was undergoing a puritan purge. After a brief spell of exile from Geneva, he returned in 1541 and set about reforming the city. Theologically, Calvin believed in predestination and opposed papal supremacy or any practices not prescribed by the Bible. Politically, he had a much greater impact. He reorganized life in Geneva, setting up an assembly of pastors and elders to sit in judgment on the morals of their neighbors. People might be called before the assembly for bad conduct, and penalties for frivolous behavior could be severe. Gambling, swearing, and dancing were banned, while taverns and sexual morality were regulated. Drunkenness, blasphemy, and agnosticism carried the same penalty as murder. Along with the new puritan ideals went a dedication to commerce, and as a result Geneva flourished. Calvin died in 1564, leaving behind a wealthy but austere city.

LANGUAGE

SWITZERLAND SITS AT THE VERY POINT where three other major cultural regions meet. But its mountainous landscape has meant that whole communities have remained separated and isolated for generations. Consequently, it has four national languages and many regional variations so strong that, in some cases, people speaking dialects of the same language cannot understand one another.

Approximately 64 percent of the country speaks some variant of Swiss-German as their mother tongue, 19.2 percent French, 7.6 percent Italian, 0.6 percent Romansh, and almost 9 percent some other language. The last group consists of foreign workers who come from Spain, Portugal, or elsewhere. As with the religious makeup of the country, the language groups are not as clearly defined by geography as they once were. Communities of each language group live in all the cities.

Above: **People engage in conversation at an outdoor café in Geneva. The majority of Swiss speak some form of German.**

Opposite: **Road signs point the way in the Alps in the canton of Valais.**

NATIONAL AND OFFICIAL LANGUAGES

Switzerland has problems when standard items like official documents, banknotes, or street signs have to be understood by all its citizens. Switzerland has alleviated this problem to a certain extent by having three official languages: German, French, and Italian. All banknotes and official documents are written in all three languages. In addition, Romansh was made a national language in 1938 and was later accorded the status of semiofficial language in a 1996 referendum. Romansh appears on official documents that are used in Romansh areas, and it is always the formal form of address in areas where the language is spoken.

A sign prohibits camping in four languages: German, French, English, and Italian.

EVOLUTION OF LANGUAGES The Romansh language evolved in Switzerland when the Rhaeti came into contact with the conquering Romans.

German came to the area with the Alemanni. Swiss German, based on the language spoken by the Alemanni, evolved along different lines to the standard German spoken in Germany.

French came much later when the Burgundians gradually adopted Latin, and this mixture eventually evolved into French.

Later, the situation was complicated by the groups of German-speaking Protestants who settled in the French-speaking Jura. Romansh disappeared from the Rhine valley and was replaced by German, and various patois forms of French developed in the Valais, Jura, and Fribourg areas.

GERMAN AND SWISS GERMAN

As we have already seen, the German spoken in Switzerland evolved separately from the High German used as the standard language in Germany. Some of its grammatical structure and vocabulary are different from the German spoken in Germany, while its pronunciation is often quite different from Germany's. In addition, Swiss German has three main dialect groups, as well as many subdialects found in isolated valleys and enclaves, so that it is not always possible for the speaker of one German dialect to understand the speaker of another. The official written language used in business and by the civil service in Swiss-German-speaking cantons is High German. In

spoken communication, Swiss-German is used in most official settings, except with foreigners, when Swiss-German speakers quite easily revert to High German, spoken with a Swiss accent. This is rarely spoken, although most Swiss-German speakers understand it, read it in books and daily newspapers, and listen to it on television. News broadcasts are made in standard German, but the sports commentaries are in Swiss-German.

The Titëuf series of French comic books was authored by Philippe Chapuis, a Swiss illustrator based in France. Around 11 million copies of the books had been sold by 2004 since 1993.

FRENCH

About 18 percent of the population of Switzerland speak French, mostly in the west of Switzerland, in the cantons of Geneva, Vaud, and Neuchâtel. With French the situation is a little less complicated than with the other language groups, since there are fewer surviving dialects. Until recent years there were areas, especially around the Valais and Jura, where a dialect of French similar to Savoyard was spoken. Today, only the older people know this dialect, and it is rarely spoken.

ITALIAN AND ITS VARIATIONS

Italian is the official language of Ticino and parts of Graubünden, both relatively small areas of Switzerland. But even within such small communities, there are many different dialects of Italian spoken. Italian dialects are more mutually incomprehensible than German dialects, and there are many different dialects, some more like Lombard (a northern Italian dialect) and others closer to Romansh. The situation is complicated by the fact that even within small villages there are also Romansh and German speakers. The official form is standard Italian, used in conversations of an official nature, as well as in documents and on television. Within the same conversation, two speakers may switch between standard Italian and their common dialect as their discussion shifts between official business and more general matters.

ROMANSH

Although Romansh is spoken only by 0.6 percent of the population in Switzerland, it is one of the country's national languages and is a semi-official language. Romansh's regional center is in Coira, in the Graubünden canton. The language emerged from a combination of the languages spoken in the area before the Roman invasion and the Latin of the Roman Empire. Linguistic scholars believe the Romansh language evolved from the Etruscans, a highly sophisticated society from west-central Italy that flourished before the Roman Empire. Romansh is thought, too, to have influences from an even older Celtic language, as well as from Semitic.

There are many dialects of Romansh in Switzerland, the result of the isolation of small communities also typical of other regions of Switzerland. Of the five different dialects of Romansh, the most widely spoken is the

Sursilvan dialect. In the Engadine area of Graubünden, another dialect known as Ladin is spoken, and in central Graubünden, two dialects, Surmiran and Sutsilvan, are spoken. Romansh is also spoken in southern Tyrol in Austria.

Today all of the Romansh-speaking areas have German-speaking or Italian-speaking majorities. As schools standardize languages and television dominates life, maintaining every single dialect as a living language becomes harder with each generation. The fact that there are so many different versions of Romansh makes the survival of the language even less likely. The younger generation of Swiss writers from the Graubünden has in recent decades been developing a steadily growing interest in writing fiction in Romansh. One of the more renowned writers of fiction was Flurin Spescha (1958–2000). Public efforts toward the promotion of trilinguism, a Romansh press, and television and radio broadcasts in Romansh have resulted in an increased interest in preserving and maintaining the tradition of communication and literary practices in the language.

In cosmopolitan Zürich, a Swiss bank is given its name in French, Italian, and German.

WHAT'S IN A NAME?

With four national languages, giving things a name that everyone understands can be a difficult activity. Even the major cities are called by different names, depending on what region of Switzerland you are in. The name of the country itself varies according to its languages, being known as Schweiz (German), Suisse (French), Svizzera (Italian), and Svizra (Romansh). The lakes have different names altogether, depending on which language you use. For instance, that lake that we call Lake Geneva is known to German-speakers as Genfersee and to French speakers as Lac Léman.

THE MEDIA

Switzerland publishes just over 11 newspapers per 1 million people, which secures it the 10th place in the list of countries with the most newspapers per capita. This list is dominated by small countries, with the mini-countries San Marino, Gibraltar, and Andorra topping the rankings.

There are 81 different newspapers in Switzerland, not including free newspapers or official gazettes. These newspapers have a total circulation of 2.7 million.

In Switzerland there are 115 television broadcast stations and a total of 119 radio broadcast stations. There are a total of 7.1 million radio sets and 3.3 million television sets owned in the country. The Swiss can listen to several international French-speaking and German-speaking channels, and Swiss television offers programs in Italian and Romansh.

BIEL

Biel is a town on the shores of Lake Biel, a few miles from the better known Lake Neuchâtel. It is an industrial town, but it also attracts a fair number of tourists. It is a particularly interesting place as far as languages go, because its citizens are more or less evenly distributed between French speakers and German speakers, and it is Switzerland's only officially bilingual town. Many of its citizens are bilingual, speaking both languages well. Here one may hear both languages on and off in the same conversation, as the speakers change topics. Not surprisingly, the town itself has two names, Biel and Bienne, while the lake next to it is called either Lac de Bienne or Bieler See.

ARTS

IN THE MOVIE *The Third Man*, made just after World War II, Harry Lime, the central character, cynically defends violence by claiming that Italy, in 50 years of war and mayhem under the rule of the Borgias, managed to produce great works of art, while all Switzerland managed to produce in 500 years of peace and democracy was the cuckoo clock.

That is an unfair description of Switzerland, but strangely, it is the image that many people believe characterizes Switzerland—a safe but dull place that produces only safe but dull things.

Above: **The opera house in Geneva. Although Switzerland is not a leading center of European culture, it has a very active and varied cultural life, as well as many fine museums and theaters.**

Opposite: **A statue of famous comedian Charlie Chaplin stands in Vevey, in the canton of Vaud, where he lived during the last years of his life.**

In reality, Swiss art forms are dynamic and varied, and Switzerland's safety has convinced many artists to settle there. Switzerland has productive theaters, orchestras, and artists.

Part of Switzerland's image problem is caused by its three major languages. Because Swiss writers use French, German, or Italian, they become part of the school of literature of France, Germany, or Italy rather than of Switzerland itself.

It is the same for other fields of artistic endeavor. Many famous Swiss personalities, such as the architect Le Corbusier or the painter and sculptor Alberto Giacometti, are considered French or Italian, despite the fact that they were Swiss-born.

FINE ARTS

Switzerland has produced some of Europe's most famous artists. In the 18th century, Jean-Étienne Liotard and Salomon Gessner produced many worthwhile works of art, while Angelika Kauffmann was active in Europe. In the 19th century, Leopold Robert was famous for his paintings of Italian life. Arnold Böcklin, a painter who worked at the turn of the century, painted symbolic pictures depicting tortured passion. Ferdinand Hodler is considered the father of Swiss landscape painting and did his best work at the turn of the century. He also produced many frescoes depicting events in Swiss history. In the 20th century, the painter Giovanni Giacometti developed a Postimpressionist style, while his cousin Augusto Giacometti used colors in an innovative way in his landscape paintings. Félix Vallotton created his own distinctive style of painting—a very bold realism. The famous architect Le Corbusier was also Swiss, although little of his architectural designs can be found in Switzerland. He is also famous for his paintings and, with French artist Amédée Ozenfant, created a new school of art called Purism.

Perhaps the most famous Swiss artist of all is Paul Klee, who studied art in Munich and later settled in Germany, forming part of the Der Blaue Reiter (The Blue Rider) group. He taught at the Bauhaus, a German design school, and in 1932 returned to Switzerland during the rise of Fascism in Germany. Many of his paintings were confiscated by the Nazis. He continued his work in Switzerland, creating small-scale oil paintings such as the abstract *Twittering Machine*, which is now in New York City.

Paul Klee's painting *Possibility on the Lake* expresses his philosophy that painting should convey the essential spiritual significance of things and not just the familiar reality.

The famous Dada artists emerged from post-World War I Zürich. The name, chosen at random from a French-German dictionary, is a French word meaning hobby horse. The Dadaists challenged the established rules of art and used shock tactics to make people think differently about art. There were only a few Swiss artists in the group, but they (especially Jean Arp) are still considered an important part of the movement. Apart from Zürich, Dadaism also flourished in cities abroad, such as New York City, Paris, Berlin, Cologne, and Hannover.

Alberto Giacometti, the son of the Impressionist painter Giovanni Giacometti, also achieved world fame as a painter and sculptor. The Swiss-born artist studied art in Geneva from 1919 to 1920. He then left for Italy, where he was inspired by collections of Egyptian art. He resumed his studies in Paris, where he produced most of his work. In the 1930s he became part of the Surrealist movement and produced abstract symbolic works. His final style consisted of "thin man" statuettes cast in bronze.

Recently, young Swiss artists have begun to explore some dynamic new ideas. Ugo Rondine depicts a sense of the ego in his abstract paintings, while Dieter Wymann takes everyday pieces of furniture and breaks them apart, reassembling them in ways that make one consider the meaning of familiar objects. Albrecht Schneider paints family groups that challenge accepted ideas of formal group paintings. He uses bright colors and arranges his figures in ways that seem to question the security of the family group.

A house designed by Le Corbusier, who was one of the main creative forces behind the International school of architecture that influenced 20th-century building trends in the West.

SWISS ARCHITECTURE

One way of tracing the developments in Swiss architectural styles is through the religious buildings. The earliest style found in Switzerland is the Romanesque. Churches in this style were built in the Middle Ages. In Switzerland, the style is characterized by either barrel-vaulted ceilings (round railway tunnel-type ceilings) or by flat-ceilinged bare rooms supported by pillars.

Later, this simple design was replaced by the Gothic style. The vaulted ceiling became more complex, and highly ornate altars, as well as heavily carved and ornamented furniture, began to make an appearance. There are many Gothic churches throughout Graubünden and in the German-speaking parts of Switzerland.

From the 17th century, a complex, highly ornate new style called Baroque emerged. The Counter-Reformation had begun, and many cantons that had converted to Protestantism were returning to Catholicism and its elaborate church design. Walls were covered in frescoes and paintings. Gilded and carved screens filled the interiors, and paintings of the

Virgin Mary and the saints appeared. Elaborate baroque churches can be found in Einsiedeln and Saint Gall.

In contrast, the modern architectural style is stark and uses reinforced concrete to good effect. An example of this style is the Church of Saint Anthony in Basel designed by Karl Moser.

The most famous Swiss architect is Le Corbusier. He did most of his work in Paris and, later, in Germany. Le Corbusier developed a theory of the relationship between modern machine forms and architectural technique. His buildings are typically raised on stilts. He planned areas of the cities of Algiers, Buenos Aires, and Chandigarh, and his influence can be seen in city planning and architecture all over the world.

Above and opposite: **The exterior and interior of the Council House in Basel. Built in the Gothic style, the building was completed in the early 16th century.**

97

REGIONAL ARCHITECTURE

Every canton in Switzerland has its own distinctive style of house. In the mountains around Bern, houses have low pitched roofs, with wide overhanging eaves tiled with wooden shingles held in place by stones. The outside of the house is covered in pastoral art, with decorated and carved beams and pillars. This is the typical Swiss chalet of the tourist brochures. In the lowland region of Bern, the houses have an enormous roof reaching down to the second-story windows, which creates a large covered area around the house (below).

In the Appenzell region, it rains a great deal and the domestic architecture is designed to deal with this type of weather. The houses and their outbuildings are built in a continuous row so that the inhabitants do not have to walk around in the rain. They have cellars, and the roof shingles often cover the walls too. The gable end of the house always faces the valley.

Around Lucerne the houses are usually four or five stories tall, and a steep roof covers the top stories, producing dormer windows (windows projecting from the roof). The front door to the house is on the second story and is approached by means of an outdoor staircase.

In the Valais, the houses are again four or five stories high and built of wood. The kitchen is

usually in a separate building made of stone, attached to the main building by a covered walkway. Long balconies run along the length on one side of the house.

In the Italian-speaking Ticino region, houses are very simple. They are stone-built with thick walls to support roof tiles made from stone slabs. The staircases to the upper floors are usually on the outside of the house.

PRINTING

Swiss craftsmanship and artistry meet in Swiss printing. Since the Reformation, the Swiss have led in this area. In the 16th century Hans Holbein, Niklaus Manuel, and Tobias Stimmer began a tradition of drawing and printmaking by engraving wood that was then inked and printed. The cut grooves in the wood came out clear on paper while the uncut surfaces created the design or picture.

This technique continued until the 19th century, when the engraving plates were made of copper with a steel coating. Jean Arp, one of the original Dada artists, produced engravings, as did Marc Chagall, the Russian painter and designer, and Henry Moore, the English sculptor and graphic artist.

FOLK ART

In a country with so strong a rural tradition as Switzerland, it stands to reason that there should be strong and vibrant folk art. This can be seen in many of Switzerland's folk museums, where displays include the carved and painted farming implements used for the traditional journey to the high pastures in spring.

More characteristic are the *Sennenstreifen* (sen-nen-SCHTRY-fen), long strips of paper or wood painted in a primitive style and showing the movement of cattle to the high pastures. The pictures often show long lines of cattle, mountains, farm buildings, and herdsmen in traditional costume. These painted strips were hung over the door to the cowshed or even in the living room. In eastern Switzerland the tradition was for *Senntum-Tafelbilder* (sen-toom TAHH-fell-bill-dare). These are small paintings of similar motifs usually executed in watercolors on cardboard or paper.

Opposite, top and bottom: **Traditional buildings in the Bernese Alps and the Bernese Mittelland, in the canton of Bern. Every geographical region of Switzerland has its own architecture and home decor styles.**

SWISS LITERATURE

Some of Hesse's more mature writings, such as *Demian,* a novel about troubled adolescence, were influenced by his interest in psychological studies, in particular those of Jung.

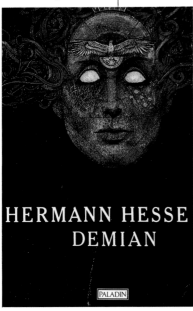

With three different official languages and a host of dialects, as well as Romansh, Switzerland has a varied and interesting literary history. As a neutral and safe state, Switzerland also has been home to many non-native people who wrote in the Swiss languages.

Switzerland can claim some famous names in literature. Jean-Jacques Rousseau was born in Geneva and spent most of his life there until 1742, when he went to live in Paris and became famous. Hermann Hesse was born in Germany but spent most of his life in Switzerland, where he wrote his major works. While living in Switzerland he was awarded the Nobel Prize for Literature in 1946.

In the second half of the 20th century, two Swiss playwrights writing in German became world-renowned for their works that portrayed Swiss society as restricting and complacent. Max Frisch's major works, mainly written after 1945, were influenced by the years he spent living in an isolated and neutral Switzerland during World War II. Friedrich Dürrenmatt's plays include *The Visit*, which has become a modern classic of world drama. Dürrenmatt's many works challenge the complacent qualities he saw in Swiss society, which he felt was too restrictive. Dürrenmatt died in 1990, and Frisch, a year later.

Writing in French in modern times are novelists and poets such as Gustave Roud, Blaise Cendrars, Corinna Bille, and Monique Saint-Hélier.

Italian-Swiss writers have also become famous throughout Europe, notably Felice Filippini. Giovanni Orelli, Fabio Pusterla, and Grytzko Mascioni have also made their mark.

The situation for Romansh literature is more complex as it has five dialects. It did, however, flourish in the 19th century. Noted writers include Cla Biert, Flurin Darms, and Tina Nolfi.

A portrait of Erasmus by Hans Holbein. Erasmus is credited with the revival of learning and was a proponent of the belief in humanism.

ERASMUS (1469–1536)

Desiderius Erasmus was a Dutchman who lived in the 15th century. Although not born Swiss, he lived several years in Switzerland, and many of his important works were written there. He began his life as a monk and later became secretary to the Bishop of Cambrai. He moved from Paris to England but settled eventually in Basel where he wrote his greatest masterpiece, *Colloquia,* which dealt with the wrongs of the Church.

The writings of Erasmus, covering a wide variety of topics, rank him as one of the greatest scholars of his time. The *Adagia*, published in 1508 and containing more than 3,000 proverbs collected from the works of the classical authors, established his reputation. Besides being a noted scholar, Erasmus was also the first editor of the Greek version of the New Testament.

GREAT SWISS THINKERS

Switzerland has produced a large number of people who have made important contributions in the arts and sciences. Five internationally famous Swiss personalities are Jean-Jacques Rousseau, Ferdinand de Saussure, Carl Gustav Jung, Jean Piaget, and Denis de Rougemont.

JEAN-JACQUES ROUSSEAU (1712–78) Philosopher, writer, and political theorist, Rousseau *(right)* made his outstanding contribution to political philosophy with the publication of *The Social Contract*. This work contains virtually all of Rousseau's political theory. His social and political ideas inspired the leaders of the French Revolution as well as the Romantic generation of the late 18th century. But because the Bern government disapproved of his beliefs, he was forced to leave Switzerland. Rousseau was to live in France for much of his life.

FERDINAND DE SAUSSURE (1857–1913) Saussure renewed lingustic and literary studies and was the father of structuralism, an important critical tool for all humanistic and social sciences today. He was an instructor at the School of Advanced Studies in Paris and was professor of Indo-European linguistics, Sanskrit, and general linguistics at the University of Geneva.

CARL GUSTAV JUNG (1875–1961) A Swiss psychiatrist, Jung *(left)* studied medicine at Basel University, and once he had qualified began to specialize in mental disorders, working first of all at the Burghölzli Asylum of the University of Zürich. In 1907 Jung met Sigmund Freud, already world-famous for his radically new psychological theories. The two began a close collaboration. In 1912 Jung published *Psychology of the Unconscious*. This book caused a rift between Jung and Freud, because Jung disagreed with Freud's theory that neurosis had sexual bases. Jung introduced into psychology the terms introvert and extrovert that are commonly used to describe shy, withdrawn people and outgoing, sociable people. Jung ultimately broke with Freud when he devised an alternative theory of the libido that stressed the will to live rather than sexual drive as the prime human driving force.

JEAN PIAGET (1896–1980) Piaget has had an important influence on the school life of most American children as well as children from other parts of the world. At the University of Neuchâtel, he studied zoology and philosophy, receiving his doctorate in 1918. Soon afterward he became interested in psychology and went to Zürich and Paris to study. His ideas on psychology were centered on the way the human infant learns to recognize objects in the world around it and to interact with them. He believed that as each child develops it goes through various stages: the first being physical, as it learns motor skills; the second being intellectual, as it learns language; the third involving more complex skills, such as understanding logic and the concepts of time and numbers; and the fourth involving the manipulation of abstract ideas and orderliness of thinking. Piaget's ideas have influenced educators all over the world.

DENIS DE ROUGEMONT (1906–85) Rougemont was a writer and philosopher whose work profoundly influenced the study of humanities in the 20th and 21st centuries. He produced numerous works, including *Misdeeds of the State Education*. In this work Rougemont denounced the country's education system, which he deemed as conformist.

SWISS FILM

The Swiss film industry has come a long way since its early days. A Swiss actor who became famous in European movies is Michel Simon, whose career spanned the years from the early 1930s up to 1971. He starred in screen classics such as *Boudu Saved from Drowning* (1932) and *L'Atalante* (1934), a masterpiece directed by the famous French movie director Jean Vigo. Perhaps the most famous Swiss actress is Ursula Andress, who appeared in the James Bond movie *Dr. No,* a cinema classic. Another well-known actor is Bruno Ganz, who is known both in Europe and the United States and has worked with directors such as Wim Wenders and Werner Herzog. Ganz acted as Hitler in the 2004 movie *Der Untergang.*

The small Swiss movie industry has blossomed, producing successful international movies such as Alain Tanner's *Années Lumières* (*The Light Years*), which won the Jury Prize at the Cannes Film Festival in 1981. In German, the critically acclaimed movies have been documentaries, while in French, fiction has dominated. In 1991 Xavier Koller's movie *Reise der Hoffnung* (*Journey of Hope*) won an Oscar. The movie depicted the problems of the enormous number of refugees flooding Europe. The fate of refugees is also highlighted in Joakim Demmer's *Tarifa Traffic*, which was released in 2003. The movie depicts the dangerous and often tragic sea journey that African immigrants make to cross into Europe.

"Man was born free, and everywhere he is in chains."

—Jean-Jacques Rousseau, The Social Contract

IF THERE IS a single national pastime in Switzerland, it is sports. The country has developed an amazing variety of winter and summer sports that fill the leisure hours of Swiss citizens and, as a bonus, attract thousands of tourists each year.

Skiing is one of the most widely enjoyed winter activities of Swiss citizens, who seldom have to travel far to enjoy the sport. The mountains also provide bobsledding, tobogganing, mountain walking, and climbing, and in summer, camping. Shooting is another popular activity. Every Swiss man keeps his military-issued rifle at home and uses it for shooting practice.

Above: **Men play a game of chess in a park.**

Opposite: **Switzerland has many snow-clad mountains, and the Swiss enjoy the sports that these slopes permit, such as skiing and tobogganing.**

In addition to the internationally recognized sports that are popular in Switzerland, there are also some local sports that still make their appearance at the many Swiss festivals. These are Swiss wrestling, and farmer's tennis, or *hornussen* (horh-NOOS-ehn), a game similar to baseball but played with disks instead of balls.

Other leisure pursuits include traditional activities such as folk dancing, yodeling, Alpenhorn playing, and attending concerts and the theater. The Swiss workday is one of the longest in Europe, and to balance this off, the Swiss indulge in their leisure activities with relish.

Children take skiing lessons at a ski school in a village.

SKIING

Skiing is a major tourist attraction in Switzerland and the number of places to ski and the varieties of skiing available are countless. The most popular area is probably the Bernese Alps, where experienced skiers can reach the slopes of the Eiger, Mönch, Jungfrau, and Wetterhorn mountains. Scattered throughout the region are huts with cooking facilities and bunks where skiers can rest overnight as part of a long skiing trip. A mountain railway carries skiers and their equipment into the area and makes the farthest peaks accessible. In winter, after the first snowfalls and the danger of avalanches recedes, railway stations are crowded with whole families setting out for a weekend of skiing.

Another region with limitless scope for climbing, ski races, or leisurely travel on skis is the Valais, in the southwestern part of the country. High slopes in the region include the Matterhorn, one of the best-known mountains in Switzerland. Snow lies in this area all year round, and it is a popular place with the Swiss.

Skiing

Skiing can be as expensive or as economical a hobby as each person cares to make it. Places like Saint-Moritz and Davos attract world-famous celebrities, and a stay at some of the resorts there is very expensive. The cost of buying all the latest equipment, as well as the cost of ski lessons, can be high.

A much more popular and less expensive form of skiing is *langlaufing* (LAHNG-loy-fink), the Swiss name for cross-country skiing. It requires much less skill, and therefore less instruction, and the trails are freely available to all, eliminating the high resort fees.

Every year in March, thousands of skiing enthusiasts gather in the Engadine region of Switzerland for the Engadine Ski Marathon, a 26-mile (42-km) course that stretches from Maloja, past the Engadine lakes, to Zuoz. In addition to the 13,000 people who take part, many thousands more line the course to watch the competition.

Summer skiing is another popular leisure activity in Switzerland, although, strictly speaking, this is not snow skiing but glacier skiing. The ski routes travel along the Swiss glaciers that keep their top layer of snow all year round. The activity is usually confined to the early part of the day, since the glacier surface begins to melt by about lunchtime.

Some interesting variations have been developed on the basic theme of sliding along on skis. One is ski-joring, where the skier is pulled along on skis by jeep, horse, or even airplane. Another is ski-hang-gliding, where the glider takes off with skis attached to his or her feet and uses the skis to assist in landing.

Constructed in 1898, the Gorner Grat Railway leads from Zermatt at 5,315 feet (1,620 m) above sea level to the Gorner Grat at 10,270 feet (3,130 m).

TOBOGGANING

This is a sport that developed in the late 19th century. The first toboggan run in Switzerland was created in 1885 by a group of vacationers from England. They tramped back and forth on a slope to compact the snow. Then they used buckets to carry snow to build the banks. The slope was ready after nine weeks of hard work.

In its early stages, the toboggan was a wooden sled with iron strips fixed to the bottom, and the riders sat upright as they slid down the makeshift runs. Later the toboggans began to take on a more aerodynamically sound design, and the riders learned that they could achieve greater speed if they lay flat. By the early 20th century, tobogganers were achieving speeds of 60 miles per hour (97 km per hour), and resorts were building complicated toboggan runs in order to attract an influx of people who had heard about the new sport. In 1928 the Winter Olympics were held in Saint-Moritz, and the toboggan run became one of the events.

Today, the most famous toboggan run is the Cresta Run at Saint-Moritz. The run consists of a series of hairpin bends along a steep ice channel. The slope has a total drop of 514 feet (157 km), and riders can reach a speed of 80 miles per hour (130 km per hour). The Cresta Run is built from scratch every year and is open from December to February.

Opposite top: **A curling practice session. Curling is played on many frozen lakes in Switzerland.**

Opposite bottom: **A friendly game of ice hockey.**

Below: **The Cresta Run belongs to the Saint-Moritz Tobogganing Club. Members of the club included celebrities such as Charlie Chaplin, Errol Flynn, and Brigitte Bardot.**

CRESTA RUN

CURLING

This winter sport is played by two teams of four players who each slide two curling stones on ice toward a target. A stone is rounded on the bottom so it moves easily on ice, has handles of different colors for opposing teams, weighs 40 pounds (15 kg) and is 12 inches (30 cm) across and 4 to 5 inches (10 to 13 cm) high.

The target, called a house, is a 12-foot (3.5-m) circle with a smaller circle at its center. The object is to get the stones as close to the center as possible, and scoring is based on the position of the 16 stones after all the players have had their turn. Each player has two throws alternating with a player from the opposing team. The player's skill lies in the way he or she gets the stone to follow a curved path. Team players improve the stone's direction by using a broom to sweep the ice in front of the stone as it travels. There are complex rules covering penalties and scoring. Curling made its debut in the Winter Olympics in 1998. Switzerland won the men's gold medal for that event.

OTHER WINTER SPORTS

Ice-skating is the second most popular sport in Switzerland. There are many ice-skating rinks in the country, along with naturally occurring lakes where skating is practiced. Ice hockey is a national pastime, and most towns with a rink have an ice hockey team.

SUMMER ACTIVITIES

Although Switzerland's fame is as a winter sports haven, the Swiss take part in many other sports. For instance, there are many international tennis tournaments throughout summer, attended by world-famous tennis stars. Much of Switzerland's territory is made up of lakes, and there are many different watersports available for enthusiasts. Hiking and cycling are also frequent activities.

Many traditional pastimes are held during summer. One of these is Swiss-style wrestling, which takes place in a circular pit and has its own special rules. The two wrestlers wear short linen, leather, sackcloth, or cotton shorts over their everyday pants. The two men grasp each other's torso, with the object of lifting their opponent off the ground, the first man to do so winning the match. Matches often attract as many as 300 contestants and a few thousand spectators.

Swiss farmer's tennis, or *hornussen,* is played on a large field with long wooden bats and a wooden disc instead of a ball. The fielders have to catch the disk with wooden rackets.

Another traditional Swiss game is *unspunnen stein* (oon-SPOON-en stain), or stone-putting. A player lifts a heavy egg-shaped stone over his head and throws it as far as possible. The sport requires enormous strength.

Two contestants compete in a Swiss-style wrestling match. The main event is the Federal Wrestling Festival, which takes place every three years.

Rifle shooting and gymnastics are two popular pastimes. Around one-third of the male population of Switzerland is involved in one of these two activities. Restaurants and cafés often display trophies garnered from local shooting or gymnastics events.

A local game in Switzerland played by children is *schlagball* (SHLAG-bawhl). This game is popular in the canton of Thurgau. It is similar to American softball, except that there are four bases instead of three. There is no pitcher or catcher; the batter throws the ball up and hits it before running around the bases. Another game played by Swiss children is similar to team dodge ball. Two teams face each other across a rectangular field and attempt to eliminate the other team's players by hitting them with the ball.

SOCIAL LIFE

The Swiss are essentially a home-loving people. Evening activities in Switzerland tend to end early. The last movie screening begins around 8 P.M., and many parts of most cities are still and quiet by midnight. For many people, relaxing means sitting in a café with a newspaper and a glass of wine or beer, and perhaps a plate of ham or sausage. All the cafés supply newspapers, and newspapers are often found piled on street corners next to a coin box for the honest customers to drop in their money.

In Switzerland there are groups that campaign against alcohol, and many restaurants do not serve it. Gambling, too, is frowned upon. There

are casinos, but there are no places like Las Vegas. The commonest form of gambling is *boule* (BOOL), a kind of roulette. The maximum stake allowed is 5 Swiss francs ($4), which makes it very difficult for anyone to win—or lose—a fortune. The Federal Act on Casinos came into effect on April 1, 2000. The act regulates gambling and the operation of casinos in the country. Its main aims are to ensure safe gambling and to reduce, as much as possible, the negative effects that gambling has on society.

Much of Swiss social life revolves around the family. Friends and family often get together at one another's homes rather than go out to eat. Concerts are very popular, and many Swiss people take an active part in summer performances that feature folk singing. There are many choral societies, and yodeling clubs exist where men practice the Alpine art of yodeling, raising the voice suddenly from one pitch to another. Whereas in other countries traditional costumes, dances, and singing exist primarily for the tourists, the Swiss have genuine interest in these aspects of their heritage and their festivals are not tourist-oriented.

FESTIVALS

SWITZERLAND HAS MANY FESTIVALS that are related to events in the Christian calendar, the passage of the seasons, or events in Switzerland's history. They are colorful and yet sedate; the Swiss like to observe ancient customs but deplore waste or excess.

In 1991 Switzerland celebrated its 700th anniversary as a confederation, but four years previously, people in several of the central cantons voted against any spectacular displays since these would be environmentally harmful and extravagant. As a result, the year-long celebrations were marked by small festivals in each village, with displays of traditional Swiss skills such as yodeling and flugelhorn playing, exhibitions, and concerts rather than any huge centralized displays or celebrations.

There are over 100 different festivals celebrated in Switzerland. Many originated in a pagan time before the arrival of Christianity, and this can be seen in their rituals, which include driving away evil spirits, seeking blessings for the harvest, or driving away the last of winter.

Left: **In Küssnacht village, participants in enormous bishop's miters (official headdresses) take part in a procession to celebrate Saint Nicholas' Day.**

Opposite: **In Zürich, musicians dressed in traditional clothes take part in a parade during Sechselauten, a spring festival.**

Above: **Dressed in black and red costumes, three Santa Clauses entertain to raise money for charity.**

Opposite: **Participants in a procession take a break.**

RELIGIOUS FESTIVALS

In common with other European countries, Switzerland's religious calendar begins on December 6, when the feast of Saint Nicholas is celebrated. The tradition of giving gifts, which has moved over to Christmas Eve, began with this saint's day. Saint Nicholas is the patron saint of youth, and gifts are given in honor of his generosity.

In Küssnacht, processions are held with participants wearing huge hats or bishop's miters illuminated from the inside. Festivities carry on through the night, with people celebrating in bars and wandering the streets cracking whips, blowing horns, and ringing bells. Christmas time in Switzerland has much of the glitter and celebration of an American Christmas.

The next event in the Christian calendar is Lent, a time when Switzerland abounds with festivals, the origins of most of which are completely lost. In villages around Lötschental, people dress up in hideous masks and goatskins, carry cowbells, and run around the villages making a lot of noise to scare away all the evil spirits. Other areas also celebrate their own versions of this event.

In Zürich and, especially, Basel, six weeks before Easter, tens of thousands of masked or brightly costumed celebrants take part in Fasnacht, a three-day festival similar to the New Orleans' Mardi Gras. Originally linked to the last days before Lenten abstinence, the Protestant authorities in Basel moved these days of great revelry back a week so that Fasnacht here falls in the week following Ash Wednesday.

The dramatic and colorful festival begins at 4 A.M. when all the lights in the city are turned off. Piccolos and drums then start playing in the pitch dark. Lanterns are lit, providing the only light until daybreak approaches. The masks and elaborate costumes that participants wear add to the carnival spirit. The festival continues for three days with decorated floats and more pipe-and-drum bands.

On Maundy Thursday, the eve of Good Friday, Christ's washing of His disciples' feet is celebrated in Catholic communities, and in Fribourg the bishop, as a token of humility, kisses the feet of the faithful in the cathedral.

On Good Friday there are many religious processions in the towns of southern Switzerland. In Mendrisio, a passion play is enacted on Maundy Thursday and Good Friday. On Ascension Day in Lucerne, in a ceremony dating back to 1509, priests carrying the holy sacrament ride around the village on horseback, blessing the crops.

For Corpus Christi, the streets in Appenzell are strewn with carpets of flowers. In Kippel, the Grenadiers of God march through the town in 19th-century uniforms to commemorate the event. In Romont in western Switzerland, part of the procession is a group of shrouded weeping women carrying representations of Christ's shroud, crown of thorns, and other things associated with the crucifixion.

In January, following an old custom in the Engadine, children are carried on sleds decorated with wreaths of evergreens and homemade paper roses.

FOLK FESTIVALS

In Switzerland, it is sometimes difficult to distinguish religious festivals from folk festivals since the two calendars of events have, over the centuries, become interconnected. Many of the rites have their origin in rituals much older than Christianity.

The folk festival year begins in January, when in Urnäsch, *silvesterklause* (spirits of the new year) go from house to house to wish families a prosperous year. Participants in traditional costume wear cowbells, masks, and glowing headgear that are often huge and illustrate scenes from rural life. In the middle of January in the Engadine, unmarried boys and girls in traditional costume travel in decorated sleds from one village to another. In Basel, the Vogel Gryff (Griffin) festival celebrates community ties, depicted by three symbolic figures: the wild man of the woods, a lion, and a griffin (a mythical lion with eagle's head). Accompanied by mummers, or merrymakers dressed in masks and strange costumes, the three characters mark the occasion by dancing and parading in the streets.

February sees more mummers in Basel at the Fasnacht parade, and in Schwyz, where they dress as harlequins called *blatzi*. In several villages, festivals take place in which Old Man Winter, in one form or another, is paraded through town and burned. In Zürich, the figure is a straw scarecrow called *boogg*. This symbol of winter, of which everyone is weary, is then burned by the side of Lake Zürich.

May Day is an important folk event all over Europe, and in Switzerland many small villages hold festivals. In Geneva two children, a boy and a girl, are named the May King and Queen. They are solemnly crowned on the second Sunday of May and lead a procession from house to house through their home village.

June sees the return of the cows to the high pastures in regions such as the Valais, Gruyère, and Appenzell, and this event is surrounded by many festivities. The men who herd the animals dress in traditional costume and decorate their cows with flowers and bells. There are flag-tossing competitions, Alpenhorn playing, traditional dances, and Swiss wrestling. In the lower Valais, there are cow fights in which cows are rarely harmed, but the winning cow becomes queen of the herd and wears an enormous cowbell.

Fall brings harvest festivals throughout the rural regions of Switzerland. These are accompanied by flower processions, especially in Geneva, Lugano, and Neuchâtel.

Cattle herders take their cows up to the summer pastures to feed. Both the trip up and the return to the valley give rise to much celebration.

FESTIVALS FROM HISTORY

Several of the festivals celebrated by the Swiss have their origin in some historical event. Swiss National Day, August 1, celebrates the meeting in the field at Rütli, where the first Swiss cantons forged a defensive alliance in 1291. The day is celebrated with readings of the federal pact, torchlight processions, fireworks, and bonfires throughout the country.

In July the story of William Tell is retold in Johann Schiller's 18th-century play, *Wilhelm Tell*, in Interlaken. In December Geneva celebrates the *Escalade*, which remembers the day in 1602 when the Duke of Savoy tried to conquer the city using ladders to scale the city walls. Every year, the town of Sempach celebrates the Battle of Sempach in 1386, when a small Swiss force was able to defeat Duke Leopold III of Austria. National costume is worn and the armor of the time is dusted off for the festivities.

Below: **A poster announces the date of a festival in Geneva.**

MODERN FESTIVALS

Switzerland has many festivals whose origins are recent. In 1938 Toscanini began a music festival in Lucerne, and each year world-famous orchestras and conductors come to the city to perform in the concert hall by the lake. Zürich has a music festival where the emphasis is on opera, and Montreux and Gstaad also have classical music festivals.

Zürich also holds a jazz festival and an arts festival in June, with all the arts represented. There are concerts, art exhibitions, operas, and plays in all the national languages, as well as folk music, street theater, and music. Montreux holds a very prestigious television festival, where all the European countries submit entries for the Golden Rose of Montreux Award.

FOOD FESTIVALS

Harvest is an occasion for festivals that celebrate the year's crops. In the wine-growing areas, there are many wine festivals. The one at Vevey is unusual as it is celebrated only rarely, four times in the 20th century. The festival dates back to the Middle Ages when there was a winemaker's guild. This guild awarded prizes to the best workers in the vineyards, who then paraded through the town. By the 17th century, the event had become a celebration of the wine god, Bacchus, with the god himself portrayed in the procession by a small boy seated on a barrel. Ceres, a goddess, was also represented, as were several other figures from mythology.

More recent festivals have added fife and drum bands from Basel and herdsmen from Gruyère. The last festival was in 1999 and was a very elaborate affair. Planning began six years before, and the festival involved around 5,000 people and hundreds of goats, oxen, and horses.

In the Bernese Alps, a new festival has been created by an old tradition. It was, and still is, common for the farmers of the region to pool their milk in order to make cheese. Once the cheese is ready at the end of summer, it is given out to each farmer in proportion to the milk produced by his cows. Once upon a time it may have been a simple operation, but today it has been turned into an event, with stalls selling the cheese and lots of wine and food served to the accompaniment of music.

The annual distribution of cheese is an occasion for celebration in the Bernese Alps, in Bern canton.

FOOD

SWISS COOKING IS AS VARIED as the races of the people that make up the country. It is an interesting mix of French, German, and Italian cooking with some indigenous dishes thrown in. The Swiss kitchen contains fewer convenience foods than its American equivalent, and the Swiss shop carefully for fresh vegetables in the green markets that still fill the towns and cities.

Staples vary from area to area, but the potato is ubiquitous. In the Italian-speaking Ticino area, rice is the staple, while polenta, a dish made from corn, is also popular. Switzerland is of course famous for its cheeses. It produces its own wine and many forms of dried and cured meat. The best known Swiss dish is fondue (fahn-doo), which means blended in French. Fondue is a dish of melted cheese and wine served with bread.

Above: **Fruit and vegetables are sold in the green markets of Switzerland's towns and cities. While livestock farming is confined mostly to the mountain regions, farm produce is grown in the central plateau and the lower Alpine valleys.**

Opposite: **A dairyman handles a wheel of cheese during Chästeilet, the cheese-sharing ceremony, in Sigriswil, near Bern. Cheese sharing is a 250-year-old tradition. The cheese produced on the Alps during the summer months is shared on this day in the fall.**

REGIONAL DISHES

Regionally, the cuisines of Switzerland follow the linguistic makeup of the country. In western Switzerland, cooking styles have French influence. Italian dishes predominate in the south, while the rest of the country tends to favor German cuisine. In the west, fish dishes are the speciality. Bernese salmon or many of the freshwater fish such as char, grayling, and trout are simply cooked in butter. Mushrooms are also important in western Swiss cooking, and mushroom sauce is used for a variety of dishes, such as the highly popular *Züricher geschnetzeltes* (TSUE-rish-err guh-SCNETTS-ell-tess). The west also specializes in cured pork.

In Lucerne, Zug, and other parts of central Switzerland, a popular regional dish is cheese soup. A Zürich speciality is a meat stew made from strips of meat and served with the German version of *rösti*, or pan-roasted potatoes. *Ratsherentopf* (rahts-HAIR-un-topf) is another Zürich dish made from several different stewed meats and potatoes.

In the Valais and Graubünden, dried meats are expensive and much in demand. The meat is hung in the arid air of the mountain slopes and left to dry out completely. It is not smoked. The meat is sliced very thinly and served with pickled onions or gherkins as an hors d'oeuvre.

In Bern and the Rhine cantons, veal is popular and often cooked in cream sauce and served with noodles. Another speciality is *mistkratzerli* (MIST-krahts-err-lee), a dish of young rooster served with baked potatoes. Saint Gall and Basel are famous for their own variety of sausage.

Ticino is famous for its rice and noodles, as one would expect of an Italian-speaking region. *Busecca* (boo-SECK-ka), a soup made from tripe, and a dish of snails served with walnuts are also Ticino specialities.

CAKES AND PASTRIES

The most popular cakes in Switzerland are called *leckerli* (LEKK-err-lee), which are flat and oblong-shaped spiced honey cakes topped with a coating of sugar icing. They vary from place to place, being made with bear-shaped candies on the top in Bern. *Gugelhopf* (goo-gell-HOPEF) is another regional cake that is popular all over Switzerland. It is a large bun with a hollow center that is often filled with whipped cream. *Birnenbrot* (BEER-nenn-brote) is a teabread made with dried fruit, while *fladen* (FLAH-den) and *krapfen* (KRAHP-fen) are richer fruit cakes filled with nuts, almond paste, and pears. *Kirschtorte* (KIRSH-torta) from Zug has become another national favorite. As its name suggests, it is a cherry tart. From the Engadine comes *nusstorte* (NOOSE-tore-ta), a layer cake made with nut dough.

A bakery in a French-speaking area offers all kinds of desserts including cakes and cookies.

THE POTATO

It is not only the Irish who have made great use of the potato. Arriving in Switzerland sometime in the 17th century, the potato soon became a very important part of the Swiss diet. Perhaps even more than the Irish, the Swiss have devised many delicious ways of preparing the humble potato. In Swiss cooking, potatoes are rarely served plain or even as French fries. They are cooked whole in their skins or boiled, and then pureed, piped on to baking trays, and baked to make potatoes au gratin, or they are boiled, diced, dried, and then pan-fried to make *rösti*. Potatoes are also an important element of the cheese dish *raclette* (rah-KLEHT).

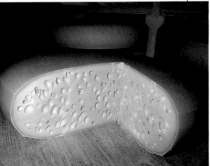

SWISS CHEESE

Swiss cheese is famous because of Emmentaler, the cheese with the large round holes running through it. But there are many types of Swiss cheeses other than this one type.

Emmentaler has its holes because of the way it is made. Over the four months that the cheese is left to ferment, it produces carbon dioxide that forms into bubbles, and as the cheese sets, the bubbles become fixed within it. Regularly shaped and perfectly round bubbles are a sign that the cheese has fermented properly. The cheese originated in the 13th century in Emmental Valley, in the canton of Bern.

Gruyère is another very famous Swiss cheese. Others are not so widely known. *Tête de Moine* is a soft cheese made in a cone-shaped block from which the cheese is scraped. *Vacherin*, a cream cheese made in the Jura, is stored in round boxes made from birchbark. It ripens during the summer and is ready by November.

Raclette is a dish made from melted Swiss cheeses, mostly *bagnes* (BAHH-nyeh) and *conches* (kahnch) cheeses made in the Valais. The cheeses are cut in half and left by an open fire to melt. When they are ready, they are poured over potatoes boiled in their skins and served with pickled spring onions and gherkins. Other popular cheese dishes are *salés au fromage* (sal-LAY oh froh-MAJJ), cheese quiche, and cheesecake.

FONDUE

The cantons of Valais, Vaud, and Geneva all claim to have originated this famous Swiss dish. The cheese is melted in a pot, which is brought to the table and kept at a bubbling temperature over a flame. Diners each have a plate of chunks of white bread that they spear on a long, two-pronged fork and dunk into the sauce. As the sauce boils away, it gets stronger and better. Traditionally, the person who lets bread fall into the pot has to buy a bottle of white wine for all the diners. One way to avoid this is to choose a cube of bread with crust on it. Tea and dry white wine are traditionally served with the fondue. Iced drinks are not advisable for consumption with warm cheese.

CHEESE FONDUE NEUCHÂTELOISE

8 ounces (250 g) Emmentaler cheese
8 ounces (250 g) Gruyère cheese
1 large clove garlic
1/2–1 cup dry white wine

2–4 tablespoons kirsch
Freshly ground black pepper
Cubes of French bread

Grate the cheeses. Rub the fondue pot or saucepan with the clove of garlic. Leave the garlic in the pot, heat the pot, and add the wine. Bring to a boil. Lower the heat and begin adding the cheese, stirring all the time with a wooden spoon. As the cheese melts, a thick sauce will develop. Add the kirsch, season with pepper, and serve, keeping the pot hot over a burner, but without letting it boil. Spear the bread cubes on long forks and dip into the sauce.

A vineyard on the shores of Lake Geneva.

SWISS WINES

Swiss wines are not as famous as French or German wines and rarely travel abroad. This is because they are in such great demand in Switzerland itself that the supply does not cover the foreign demand.

People in the west and south of the country consume more wine than people in the German-speaking areas, who consume more beer. It is thought that the grapevine was first brought to Switzerland by the Romans. Grapevine cultivation in the country, however, picked up only in the 12th century. The Swiss make mostly white wine in the Valais, Vaud, and Neuchâtel regions, where the long dry summers favor wine growing. Ticino grows mostly black grapes that make the red wines.

A 1993 statute regulates the production of both ordinary and premium wines, while alcohol in general is regulated by the Constitution.

A CULINARY CALENDAR

Many traditional Swiss dishes are linked to special times of the year. At New Year, the traditional dish in Ticino is *zampone* (zam-POHN-nee), stuffed pig's feet cooked with lentils, while in Graubünden, smoked pork with vegetables in barley soup is eaten.

Shrove Tuesday brings deep fried crisp wafers of pastry. In the canton of Ticino, whole villages bring out huge pots in which they cook risotto, stirring it constantly with enormous wooden spoons. It is served with garlic-flavored pork sausages.

At Easter, the traditional dish is lamb or kid, and it is customary for families to go off to the countryside to pick dandelion greens for their salads.

In the fall, when the shooting season starts, chamois is on the menu.

Before the use of feed grain made it possible to keep animals alive through winter, huge amounts of meat became available in the markets in the fall, and smoked and cured meats still abound during this period.

One dish common at this time in Switzerland is *bernerplatte* (BAIR-nair-PLAHT-ta), which consists of cured and smoked meats served with potatoes and sauerkraut or French green beans.

Risotto, which is rice cooked in broth and flavored with grated cheese, is also served with mushrooms.

129

RÖSTI

This recipe serves four people.

2 pounds (1 kg) large potatoes
1 quart (1 liter) water
2$\frac{1}{2}$ tablespoons butter or lard
2 teaspoons salt
1 tablespoon margarine

Boil the potatoes in the water for 20 minutes. Remove and drain the potatoes. Set them aside to cool and refrigerate for at least 4 hours. Peel the cold potatoes, then grate them. Heat the butter or lard in a medium or large frying pan and add the grated potato. Sprinkle with salt. Flatten the potatoes into a pancake shape in the pan. Cover and let sit for 15 minutes to achieve a golden crust. Spread the margarine along the edges of the frying pan, and allow it to melt. Wait a further 5 minutes, then carefully remove the rösti from the pan. Place on large plate with the crustier side on top and serve immediately.

VEAL GESCHNETZELTES

This recipe serves four people.

1.3 pounds (600 g) veal or chicken
    fillets
1 tablespoon all-purpose flour
salt and pepper to taste
2 tablespoons cooking oil
2 tablespoons butter
1 medium-sized onion, finely chopped
11 ounces (300 g) mushrooms, thinly
    sliced
1 teaspoon lemon juice
4 ounces (100 ml) dry white wine
7 ounces (200 ml) cream
1 tablespoon cornstarch
4 ounces (100 ml) beef bouillon (stock
    cube)
2 tablespoons English parsley,
    chopped

Slice the meat into thin strips. Lightly cover the meat with flour, and season with salt and pepper.

Heat the oil in a frying pan. Lightly fry the meat in small portions, making sure it develops a light crust, then put into a pre-warmed oven at 108°F (60°C).

Melt the butter in the frying pan. Add the onions, then the sliced mushrooms. Add the lemon juice, then carefully pour in the white wine to moisten the vegetables. Let this mix cook on low for a few minutes, until the fluid is slightly reduced.

Mix the cream and cornstarch together in a small to medium bowl. Add the beef bouillon and pour this mixture into the pan with the onions and mushrooms. Let this cook on low for another 3 to 5 minutes. Now add the cooked meat to this mixture, then reheat and season if needed. Sprinkle the chopped parsley on top just before serving.

This dish goes well with rice or *rösti*.

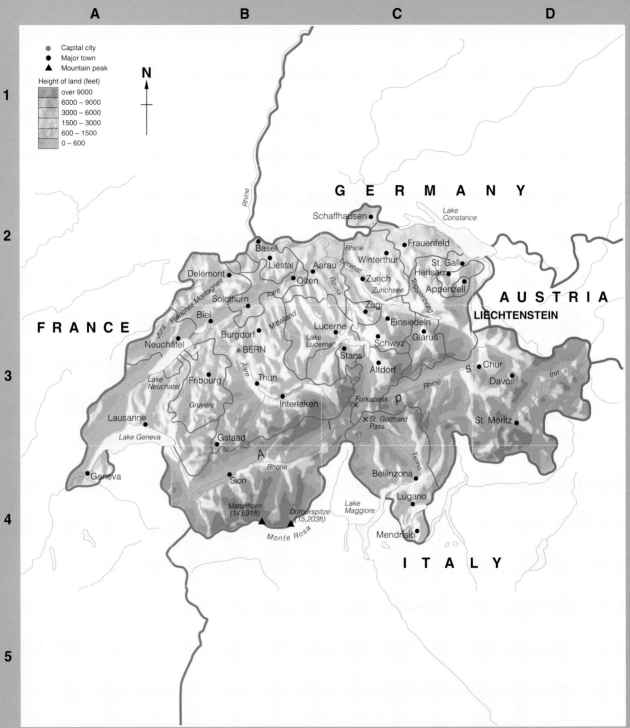

MAP OF SWITZERLAND

ECONOMIC SWITZERLAND

Manufacturing

 Chemicals

Chocolates

Electrical Appliances

Machinery Manufacturing

Pharmaceuticals

Precision Instruments

Textiles

Watchmaking

Services

Banking & Finance

Tourism

Agriculture

Grapes

Livestock

Olives

Tobacco

Vegetables

ABOUT
THE ECONOMY

OVERVIEW

While Switzerland is not particularly rich in natural resources, it enjoys one of the world's highest living standards. Inflation remains generally low and its key industries, such as the famous Swiss banking industry, keep the economy buoyant. One major problem looming in the future is the greying population. More and more people reach retirement age and the active work force is unable to provide for their social security. Some argue that Switzerland may have to loosen its immigration policies even further to deal with this problem in the coming years.

GROSS DOMESTIC PRODUCT

$239.8 billion (2003)

GDP SECTORS

Agriculture 1.5 percent, industry 34 percent, services, 64.5 percent (2003)

LAND AREA

15,938 square miles (41,290 sq km)

CURRENCY

1 Swiss franc (CHF) = 100 centimes
USD1 = CHF1.26 (July 2004)
Notes: 10, 20, 50, 100, 200, 500, 1000
Coins: 5, 10, 20 centimes; 1/2, 1, 2, 5 francs
(Since 2002 the euro is also accepted in Switzerland.)

AGRICULTURAL PRODUCTS

Eggs, fruit, grains, meat, vegetables

INDUSTRIES

Machinery, chemicals, , textiles, watches, precision instruments

EXPORTS

Machinery, chemicals, metals, watches, agricultural products

IMPORTS

Machinery, chemicals, metals, motor vehicles, textiles, oil, natural gas, agricultural products

TRADE PARTNERS

Germany, United States, Italy, France, Netherlands, United Kingdom, Austria

AIRPORTS

International airports: Zürich, Geneva, Basel Regional airports: Bern-Belp, Saint Gallen, Lugano-Agno.

INFLATION RATE

0.6 percent (2003)

LABOR FORCE

3.7 million (2003)

UNEMPLOYMENT RATE

3.7 percent (2003)

ECONOMIC AID DONOR

$1.1 billion (1995)

CULTURAL SWITZERLAND

Basel
This town boasts one of Switzerland's finest city gates, the Spalentor, which was constructed in the late 14th century as part of the town's fortification efforts. Basel is home of a medieval cathedral, which has red sandstone walls, two slender towers, and a colorful roof. The town also has an imposing City Hall, which was built from 1507–13.

Zurich Old Town
Especially appealing in Zurich Old Town are the three landmark churches: the Fraumünster, Grossmünster, and St. Peter's Church, all of which are more than 800 years old. The Grossmünster's unique twin spires are a distinct Zurich landmark. The tower clock of St. Peter's church has Europe's largest clock face with a diameter of 29 feet (8.7 m).

Benedictine Abbey of Einsiedeln
This abbey is a stunningly beautiful example of baroque architectural skills, considered by many to be Switzerland's most beautiful church building. A pilgrimage site since the Middle Ages, the newly restored abbey features the Lady Chapel with the Black Madonna.

Bern
Not only is Bern the capital of Switzerland, it also houses many interesting museums, historical arcades, and lovely old architecture. In 1191 Duke Berthold V of Zähringen named the city after the first animal—a bear—he killed in a hunt. Living bears have been kept as the city's pets since 1513. Even today there are bear pits in the center of the town.

Tell Museum
This museum in Bürglen, which is the birthplace of William Tell, contains a large collection of documents and articles of both historical and artistic character from over six centuries. The quaint, well-preserved Tell village, now part of the museum, is guarded by a tower.

Lucerne
Lucerne has breathtaking scenery and numerous medieval structures, such as the two covered bridges, Kapellbrücke (Chapel Bridge) and Spreuerbrücke (Spreuer Bridge), which span across the Reuss River. Both bridges are adorned with beautiful paintings and one even has a small chapel, built in 1568, in the middle.

Montreux Jazz Festival
This is one of the world's most respected jazz festivals and has been held every summer in the beautiful lakeside town of Montreux since 1966. Its offerings also include other styles of popular music, such as rock and rhythm and blues.

Castle of Chillon
Erected in the 13th century in Montreux, near Lake Geneva, this castle was originally a fortress but underwent many transformations over the next centuries. It was also used as a residence for the Counts of Savoy and as a state prison. The castle was made famous by Lord Byron, who wrote a poem titled *The Prisoner of Chillon* in 1816.

The Matterhorn
Though not the highest peak in Switzerland, the Matterhorn is still one of the most frequently climbed mountains in the world. Apart from mountain climbers, it attracts tourists with its unique beauty. The Matterhorn has a sharp, isolated rock pyramid with steep narrow ridges jutting from surrounding glaciers. The town of Zermatt, nestled at the foot of the mountain's northern face, became a major tourist resort mainly because of the Matterhorn.

Swiss Transportation Museum
This highly visited museum in Lucerne has all kinds of vehicles on display, such as steam and electric locomotives, railroad cars, automobiles, engines, horse-drawn coaches, bicycles, an old postal coach, antique and modern airplanes, space capsules, and aerial cable railways. It even has a space suit that was worn on the moon and lake steamers dating as far back as 1813.

ABOUT THE CULTURE

OFFICIAL NAME
Confederaziun Helvetica, or Swiss Confederation

NATIONAL FLAG
A red field with a bold, equilateral white cross in the middle that does not extend all the way to the edges of the flag.

NATIONAL ANTHEM
Schweizer Psalm (Swiss Psalm). The music and lyrics were written by Alberich Zwyssig and Leonhard Widmer, respectively. It was adopted as the national anthem in 1961.

CAPITAL
Bern

OTHER MAJOR CITIES
Zürich, Geneva, Basel

ADMINISTRATIVE REGIONS
26 cantons

POPULATION
7.45 million (2004)

POPULATION GROWTH RATE
0.5 percent (2004)

MEDIAN AGE
39.5 years (2004)

LIFE EXPECTANCY AT BIRTH
80.3 years (2004)

ETHNIC GROUPS
German 65 percent, French 18 percent, Italian 10 percent, Romansh 1 percent, other 6 percent

LITERACY RATE
99 percent (2004)

OFFICIAL LANGUAGES
German, French, Italian, Romansh

NATIONAL HOLIDAYS
New Year's Day (January 1); Epiphany (January 6); Good Friday and Easter Monday (March/April); Labor Day (May 1); Swiss National Day (August 1); Assumption (August 15); All Saints' Day (November 1); Christmas Eve (December 24); Christmas Day (December 25); New Year's Eve (December 31)

LEADERS IN THE ARTS
Arthur Honegger (composer), Bruno Ganz (actor), Paul Klee (painter), Sophie Taeuber-Arp (painter), Conrad Witz (painter), Arnold Böcklin (painter), Ferdinand Hodler (painter), Alberto Giacometti (painter and sculptor), Max Frisch (writer), Friedrich Dürrenmatt (writer), Adolf Muschg (writer), Denis de Rougemont (writer), Ferdinand de Saussure (linguist) Johanna Spyri (writer and creator of the well-known story for children, *Heidi*)

TIME LINE

IN SWITZERLAND	IN THE WORLD
20,000 B.C.–4,000 B.C. Neanderthals populate Neuchâtel.	
5th–1st centuries B.C. Celts establish La Tène civilization.	
	753 B.C. Rome is founded.
	116–17 B.C. The Roman Empire reaches its greatest extent, under Emperor Trajan (98–17).
58 B.C. Julius Caesar defeats Helvetii Celts and establishes a long period of Roman rule over much of present-day Switzerland.	
A.D. 400 Germanic people move into Switzerland after the Roman Empire's collapse.	**A.D. 600** Height of Mayan civilization
5th–1st centuries A.D. Switzerland comes under control of the Franks and later becomes part of Charlemagne's Holy Roman Empire.	
	1000 The Chinese perfect gunpowder and begin to use it in warfare.
1291 Three cantons sign a common defence treaty and found the Swiss Confederation.	
	1530 Beginning of trans-Atlantic slave trade organized by the Portuguese in Africa.
	1558–1603 Reign of Elizabeth I of England
	1620 Pilgrims sail the *Mayflower* to America.
	1776 U.S. Declaration of Independence
1797–98 Under Napoleon Bonaparte, French forces invade Switzerland and replace the Confederation with the Helvetic Republic.	**1789–99** The French Revolution

IN SWITZERLAND	IN THE WORLD
1815 After Napoleon's defeat, the Congress of Vienna restores the former Swiss Confederation and recognizes Swiss armed neutrality as a permanent policy. **1850** Rapid industrialization makes Switzerland the second most industrialized country in Europe after Great Britain.	
	1861 The U.S. Civil War begins. **1869** The Suez Canal is opened.
1914–18 Switzerland remains neutral in World War I.	**1914** World War I begins.
1939–45 Switzerland is neutral in Second World War but strikes accommodations with both sides.	**1939** World War II begins. **1945** The United States drops atomic bombs on Hiroshima and Nagasaki. **1949** The North Atlantic Treaty Organization (NATO) is formed. **1957** The Russians launch Sputnik.
1959 A coalition government of four parties takes and remains in power until the present. **1971** Swiss women get the right to vote.	**1966–69** The Chinese Cultural Revolution **1986** Nuclear power disaster at Chernobyl in Ukraine **1991** Break-up of the Soviet Union **1997** Hong Kong is returned to China.
1999 Switzerland gets its first woman president, Jewish Ruth Dreifuss.	**2001** Terrorists crash planes in New York, Washington, D.C., and Pennsylvania.
2002 Switzerland joins the United Nations.	**2003** War in Iraq

GLOSSARY

Alpenhorn
Long, powerful horn of wood or bark used chiefly by Swiss herdsmen for communicating in the Alps.

boule (BOOL)
A kind of roulette.

Corpus Christi (KORH-puhs KRIS-tee)
Roman Catholic festival in honor of the Eucharist or Holy Communion.

Fastnacht (FAHS-nahkt)
A festival celebrated before the beginning of Lent.

fondue (fahn-doo)
A popular Swiss dish of melted cheese, usually flavored with white wine and kirsch, a cherry liqueur, and eaten with bread.

hornussen (horh-NOOS-ehn)
Often called farmer's tennis, this traditional Swiss sport has a vague similarity to American baseball.

Landsgemeinde (LAHNTS-geh-min-de)
The outdoor parliament held in spring when citizens vote for their representatives.

polenta (poh-LEHN-tah)
A kind of gruel made from cornmeal.

predestination
A Calvinist belief that a soul's eventual destiny, especially its place in heaven or hell, is foreordained by God.

raclette (rah-KLEHT)
Melted cheese served with potatoes.

Romansh (roh-MANCH)
Language spoken primarily in eastern Switzerland.

rösti (ROHRS-tee)
Pan-roasted potatoes.

schlagball (SHLAG-bawhl)`
Game similar to American softball.

ski-hang-gliding
Gliding with skis attached to the feet and using the skis to assist in landing.

ski-joring
Skiing while being pulled along by a horse or by vehicles, such as a jeep or airplane.

Sonderbund
Separatist league formed on December 11, 1845, by seven Catholic Swiss cantons to oppose anti-Catholic measures by Protestant liberal cantons. The term Sonderbund also refers to the civil war that resulted from this conflict.

unspunnen stein (oon-SPOON-en stain)
Swiss shot-putting—the player lifts a heavy stone over his head and throws it as far as possible.

yodel
To sing by suddenly changing from a natural voice to a falsetto and back.

FURTHER INFORMATION

BOOKS

Creech, Sharon. *Bloomability*. New York, New York: HarperTrophy, 1999.

Davis, Thomas J. *John Calvin* (Spiritual Leaders and Thinkers). Broomall, Pennsylvania: Chelsea House Publications, 2004.

Dicks, Dianne. *Ticking Along Too—Stories about Switzerland*. Basel, Switzerland: Bergli Books, 1996.

Giacometti, Alberto, Christian Klemm, Carolyn Lanchner, Kunsthaus Zurich, and Museum of Modern Art. *Alberto Giacometti*. New York, New York: Museum of Modern Art, 2004.

Hammond, Paula. *Italy and Swizerland* (Cultures and Costumes). Brookshire, Texas: Mason Crest Publishers, 2002.

Spyri, Johanna. *Heidi*. Thorndike, Maine: Thorndike Press, 2002.

Style, Sue. *A Taste of Switzerland*. London, UK: Pavilion Books, 1992.

Teller, Matthew. *The Rough Guide to Switzerland*. London, UK: Rough Guides Ltd, 2000.

Tuttle, Susan. *Inside Outlandish*. Basel, Switzerland: Bergli Books, 1997.

World Book Staff. *Christmas in Switzerland* (Christmas Around the World). Chicago, Illinois: World Book Inc., 1994.

WEBSITES

Central Intelligence Agency World Factbook webpage on Switzerland.
http://www.odci.gov/cia/publications/factbook/geos/sz.html

General information on Switzerland. www.about.ch

Geographic, sociocultural, and political information on Switzerland.
www.swissworld.org/eng/index.html?site Sect+100

Information on Switzerland's economy. www.nationmaster.com/country/sz/Economy

List of Swiss embassies abroad.
www.goabroad.com/embassy/embassy.cfm?embassy=abroad&countryID=84

Swiss consular information. www.1uptravel.com/travelwarnings/switzerland-liechtenstein.html

Swiss history. www.buschlen.ca/history.htm

Switzerland's news and information platform. www.swissinfo.org/sen/swissinfo.html

Travel guide to Switzerland. http://sg.mySwitzerland.com/en/welcome.cfm

Travel guide to Switzerland. www.traveling.ch

VIDEOS

Switzerland—Glacier Express. Lifestyle Home Video, 1995.

Touring Switzerland. Questar Inc., 1997.

BIBLIOGRAPHY

Hadley, L. *Fielding's Europe with Children*. New York: William Morrow, 1984.
Hintz, Martin. *Switzerland—Enchantment of the World*. Chicago: Children's Press, 1986.
Lye, Keith (ed). *Today's World—Europe*. New York: Gloucester Press, 1984.
Schrepfer, Margaret. *The Summit of Europe*. Minneapolis: Dillon Press, 1989.

INDEX